Gaol

a place for the confinement of people accused or convicted of a crime.

Hawk

a person who advocates an aggressive or war-like policy or one who is constantly alert to potential opportunities of personal gain.

'For the people of Wybourn, and indeed Sheffield as a whole. My parents RIP, siblings, especially my brother Billy, god rest his soul. My lads Billy & Danny, my beloved wife Wendy and everyone who ever had to 'graft' to get by'

Clyde Broughton

*'P.S. Everyone else... go f*ck yourself!'*

'One of the Strongest Kids Yorkshire has produced'

– Paul Sykes on Clyde Broughton

Gaol Hawk

'Forged in Sheffield'

Clyde Broughton with Rob Brenton

facebook.com/warcrypress
Rob Brenton (c)

Please accept my apologies for any inaccuracies in times, dates, places, people etc. None one of them are intentional, the events contained herein were some years ago now and re-visiting those memories was somewhat of a 'graft' in itself, but it all happened in one way or another, trust me.

God bless – Clyde

Gaol Hawk - Forged in Sheffield' ISBN: 978-1-912543-04-5:

All rights reserved. No part of this publication may be reproduced or transmitted in any form or by any means, including photocopying and recording, without the written permission of the copyright holder, application for which should be addressed to the publisher at warcypress@roobix.co.uk. Such written permission must also be obtained before any part of this publication is stored in a retrieval system of any nature. This book is sold subject to the Standard Terms and Conditions of Sale of New Books and may not be re-sold in the UK below the net price fixed by the Publisher. Gaol Hawk 'Forged in Sheffield' Produced by Warcry Press (part of Roobix Ltd) on behalf of Rob Brenton, Knottingley (c) 2018.

Printed and bound in Great Britain by Clays, elcograf S.p.A

Cover photo by Bill Stephenson

Cover Art by James Ryan Foreman

Find out more at: facebook.com/gaolhawk/

Author's Introduction

'LITTLE CHICAGO'

'The labyrinth of back alleys of Sheffield after the First World War meant home-grown criminals could strike and vanish with ease. Boys that had grown up in inner city poverty had evolved into gangs that turned their urban environment to their advantage. Returning soldiers, now trained to kill, found unemployment lines instead of victory parades. Some had returned with bayonets and enemy guns and decided that if 'civvy' street wouldn't pay, criminal life might.'

Sheffield is a major city in the county of South Yorkshire in the North of England. Nicknamed the "Steel City" due to its long heritage in the forging and metal industries, its motto 'Deo Adjuvante Labor Proficit' meaning 'With God's help our labour is successful', is a mantra that still runs through the veins of its citizens to this day.

At the time it was ranked the third largest city in the country by population, with around 500,000 residents, not including all the waifs, strays and drifters that flew beneath the radar. Sheffield had a rich and well documented criminal history to say the least in fact in the 1920s Sheffield was so infested with gangs that it was nicknamed 'Little Chicago', George Orwell even dubbed Sheffield 'the ugliest town in the world.' Around 500 police officers were expected to keep a lid on a population of half a million. By 1921 a good proportion of those were unemployed adult males, ones with families to feed. The munitions factories that had previously supplied the massive bombardments of the war had closed with the onset of peace. That fall in demand, combined with a global steel depression, was devastating for an city dependent on steel production. Sheffield's crowded back to back housing saw families sharing outside toilets and meant poverty and crime infected it's cobbled streets. What passed for a welfare system was not surprisingly, overwhelmed.

For many, one small glimmer of hope in such depressing times was illegal gambling. Huge sums of money were bet on the toss of a coin in a game called 'Pitch and Toss'. It required just three coins to play and had no equipment to setup and dismantle, it was cheap, quick and could easily avoid detection from the police. The number one site for those games was on the crest of hill by the name of Skye Edge. Its location meant the gangs that controlled the game could easily see any approaching police. Hundreds of people would gather to take part. The organisers of the ring took four shillings in the pound as commission. That would pay for the 'pikers' or 'crows', the lookouts that made sure the police or rival gangs were spotted in good time. In charge of the Skye Edge gambling patch was a man by the name of George Mooney, a man who enforced his patch through violence and where necessary even murder.

There was only one thing worse than a ruthless gangland boss attempting to control the city, two gangland bosses competing for control. Mooney had laid off some of his minders and henchmen and they formed a rival gang named the 'Park Brigade'. They were led by Mooney's onetime number two, Samuel Garvin. Whilst everyone else was suffering in the depths of the depression, these gangland bosses were driving Bentley saloons through the streets of Sheffield and dining out with the cities local politicians.

To bring things to a close the biggest and baddest of the local police were assembled to form a 'Flying Squad' headed up by a new inspector with a tough reputation, Percy Sillitoe. The 38-year-old Chief Constable had left England to become a trooper in the African Police. There he worked for a tough and brutal regime which kept control over the native tribes. He brought the same methods they'd employed over in Africa to bear on the gangs of Sheffield.

Sillitoe's men wore plain clothes. They were fighting men but they fought with intelligence. They hit the gangs where it hurt most. They went into the pubs, the gangs profit centres and meeting places and told the landlords to refuse gang members service. If they didn't, they'd lose their license. In due course the city had been cleaned up.

* * * *

Cut to Hillsborough 1960 and history was about to repeat itself. International competition in iron and steel in the 1970's and 80's caused a decline in those industries for Sheffield. That coinciding with the collapse of coal mining in the area lead to a new wave of criminal activity, traditionally the one industry that is truly recession proof.

On the 12th August 1960 Clyde Broughton was born in Hillsborough in the heart of the "Steel City' and quickly set about reigniting the cities rich criminal history. An early start in petty crime, led to time at Borstal and an apprenticeship in criminality with one of the area's most notorious crooks, Dave Lee. Before long robbery with violence, burglary and run-ins with his arch nemeses in CID and the infamous upholder of justice Judge James Pickles, resulted in a hefty sentence behind bars and a steep learning curve for the young Broughton.

From there Clyde's story saw him travel through the UK's prison system, where he met some of the country's most revered faces, including 54 days solitary in Wakefield

Prison alongside possibly the country's most dangerous prisoner Robert Maudsley.

Maybe Clyde was born in to the wrong era. Sheffield's has a rich history steeped in criminality stemming back to the days of Mooney and Galvin, and his quarrels with is arch nemesis (CID Officer) and Judge Pickles drawing parallels to Sheffield's days of old.

Clyde's story is interjected with many other short tales, some humorous, from that journey, including details of his long time friendship with Heavyweight Boxer Paul Sykes, troubles at the local Gypsy Camp, a life changing Machete attack and an organised pool hustle, which was filmed and premiered by documentary makers entitled 'Smoking with The Hawk'.

Please excuse any inaccuracies, some elements of the story had to be stitched together to make them flow, remembering precisely what happened all those years ago is not an easy task, but it all happened in some manner or other. In any event here is Clyde's story...

Rob Brenton

CONTENTS

Introduction - The Wheels fall off	1
Forged in Sheffield	8
'Dreams of Naughtiness'	13
Our Billy	18
Trials at Wednesday	22
Crime Apprenticeship	27
A nice little win at the bookies	36
Lyceum Jewellers	41
The Cartoon Judge	46
Gaol	52
'Soccer in the Lock-up'	58
Fraggle Rock	63
54 days Solitary	70
Free Bird	77
The Usual Suspect	83
Fattorini's	91
Back in Armley	98

Sykesy	104
Money with menaces	112
Bred for 'feytin'	117
The Horse & Lion	124
Lindholme	129
Hull & back!	134
Shanghaied	139
Sleeper	144
Life on the tick	151
Shoplifting	156
Drifting	161
The Hustle	166
The Finale	171
Machete	178
Underworld - Afterworld	185
Afterword	191

INTRODUCTION

'The Wheels Fall Off'

BANG! BANG! BANG! The front door sounded like it was about to come off its fuckin hinges. Still laid in my pit somewhere half way between sleep and reality, that morning's wake-up call wasn't the usual type.

Still half dressed after a particularly heavy night down the Springwood I leapt to my feet, the cobwebs instantly blown away. I glanced over at my battered old alarm clock midflight, it was only six in the morning, what the fuck was going on. It was early spring and still pretty dark for that time of a morning.

BANG! BANG! This wasn't one of my pals nipping round for a cuppa on his way to the dole office or the postman with one of his now regular and apparently 'important' letters, it was more serious than that and the second round of thunder confirmed it.

BANG! BANG! CRUNCH! A bobby's knock for sure, but not the typical one. The sleep had worn off and things were becoming much clearer, it was the sound of thunder being rained on the door of my own little castle on the Manor.

Luckily the solid front door, though flexing, was having none of it, too much of a match for the local constabularies battering ram, probably harvested from monkey metal in some far-off land as part of a recent cost cutting exercise, the type which Sheffield would have been proud to manufacture only a few years previous.

BANG! BANG! BANG! It was now being swung incessantly at my door, no doubt by the fattest pig who happened to be on the squad that morning, making certain it went through without delay.

CRACK! The door of number ten Noehill Road on the Manor, Sheffield, was swelling at its hinges and about to burst, a couple more huffs and puffs from that little piggy and the prefab casing might completely fall down.

I flew down the stairs, barely touching most of them along the way, kidding myself that what I was about to face would be something I could deal with, another local crook with some relatively incidental beef, a foe that I could take on, deal with swiftly and get back to my pit.

NO CHANCE! This was the Old Bill, a small army no doubt, and I was being nicked, properly nicked. I'd realised that before I'd hit the landing carpet. What I'd have given for it to be that sweaty old red-faced postman this time, I'd have signed for that 'summons' without hesitation, maybe even used my real name.

CRACK! I'd made it to the door and fumbled the key a half turn in the lock, managing to get it open before the incompetent swine's brayed it completely from its hinges.

At the other side stood a herd of baying pigs, the front row comprising of several smartly dressed CID, six in total, headed up by Rotherham's number one bastard and lead officer John Wilson. Behind him a wall of genetically cloned foot-soldiers were ready to restrain me if needed. These lot could have been made from tissue paper for all it mattered I wasn't getting past them.

I offered no resistance, like they say it would have been futile given the barricade they'd created, I wasn't going anywhere any time soon.

The dapper John Wilson gave me a look of smug content and piped up "Mr Broughton, you're being arrested for Burglary…"

There was a brief pause, the type you get in day to day dialogue when you're about to reel off a list, whether that pause actually existed or it was my conscience telling me what I already knew was coming I couldn't be sure, but it seemed to linger for an eternity.

It was dawning on me now, they hadn't pulled me on a whim, my card had been marked for some time, the bust had to have been planned to catch me on the back foot. There hadn't been any build up, sneaking suspicion or encroaching paranoia I was caught completely off guard.

Which one of my stunts was it for? I asked myself. Surely not the whole lot, that would be my saving grace, the police couldn't possibly know about all of my activities and recent scores, statistically that couldn't be the case.

Wilson continued "And two separate counts of robbery with violence."

I was done, they had me for the lot, it defied reason, not my general day to day activities but the more significant crimes I'd been involved in during my 1979 crime apprenticeship under the wing of my trusted mentor Dave Lee.

"You have the right to remain silent. You do not have to say anything, but it may harm your defence if you do not mention when questioned something which you later rely on in court. Anything you do say..." Blah, Blah, Blah, the voices blurred as my brain went into a tailspin.

I'd heard it all before, but lord knows I didn't want to hear it this time. The realisation of what was going on was now sinking in quicker than a nicked moped to the Don bed. It was unlikely I'd be back home for some time now, I was no fool, the likelihood of me getting away with a list as endless as that was slimmer than some of the entrants at the Owlerton Stadium.

CLICK! CLUNK! Wilson cuffed my hands behind my back with zero regard for my wellbeing, in fact purposely tight. I feared by the time we'd got back to the cop shop my hands would have turned blue and fallen off. Those tin shackles were cutting my wrists like a blunt knife, rough justice was being served. I knew not to complain though, it had become somewhat of an occupational hazard.

They frog marched me out of the front door, down our blocked paving and slung me in the back of the 'Jam Sandwich', standard procedure for a local toe-rag from the Manor. If I clocked my head on the sill on the way into the car then so be it, I wasn't being handled with kid gloves anymore, I had elevated into real criminality and in their eyes, though only nineteen, I was now a mister.

SLAM! The passenger door shut, and we were off at pace. Sat in the back of the cop car on my way to West Bar Police Station in the centre of Sheffield. My brain began to rattle, thoughts buzzing around the inside of my skull like flies in a jar.

What did they know? How was I linked? Who else was on their way to the nick? Who'd bubbled me or indeed us? How could I let the other guys know we were being pulled? I could have filled a book with that endless list of questions. Many of them weren't going to be that relevant if I was looking at a ten stretch, I'd simply have to get on with it.

The car pulled up abruptly outside West Bar nick and I was hoisted out by the same fat pig that had attempted to batter down my front door. He was still blowing the poor sod. The silence in that police yard like a roman amphitheatre, amplifying my inner concerns about what I would face next.

Bundled into the custody area and up to the front desk they asked me all the usual questions, confirmation of my particulars, did I have any medical issues, suicidal thoughts etc. Maybe I didn't before but I sure as fuck thought I was about to have a thrombosis at that very moment.

They directed me down to the cells where I was left to contemplate my fate, every angle I could come up with quickly counteracted by my own doubts, there wasn't going to be any easy way out of this one.

Less than half an hour passed before I was called in for interview. Two CID coppers straight out of an episode of 'The Sweeney', took me up to the interview room. I'd been arrested half a dozen times previous, half an hour was nothing; were they were hoping I'd still be half dazed from the early wake-up call, an attempt to reduce my thinking time to form an alibi. Smart tactics from good old John 'The Bastard' Wilson and his swarve side kick Price.

The lead officer named Wilson, was a real horrible bastard from Rotherham. I'd met him before, in fact in a previous tangle with the local police, he'd once thrown a typewriter at me during interrogation, they'd give you a clip back then, it was standard procedure.

He was accompanied by another copper by the name of Price, another bastard, one who really rated himself, a real wannabe 'ladies man', a good looking cunt I'll give him that, but loved himself a bit too much, and also a first-class prick. I'd weighed them up before either had opened their mouths, bad cop and even badder cop.

CLICK, CLICK! The more senior of the two detectives Wilson engaged his Parker pen into work mode without delay, again minimising my thinking time, no opening gambit just straight in at the deep end. The nib touched paper ready to detail my every word. Shit was about to get very real.

They had me bang to rights, they knew way too much. I'd been hauled in for three major crimes all at the same time, a mugging outside the bookies on the Prince of Wales Road, a burglary at the home of a local Haulage Yard owner and a smash and grab on the Lyceum Jewellers in town. The combined force of all those charges meant one thing, serious time. The chances of me getting off with all three offences were something similar to that of winning the pools, or indeed winning twelve hundred quid down the bookies on the Prince of Wales Road and getting mugged on the way home. Maybe, just maybe, I'd shake off one of the charges, even two, but all of them? I wasn't that stupid. It was damage limitation time and by that I don't mean drawing people in, naming names to lighten my load, but playing the game, playing the game just enough to be deemed cooperative. Further down the line when the judge would be waving his pointy finger at me, most likely old Chicken-neck, Judge Michael Walker or the infamous Pickles, I'd be rewarded for that, who knows. I prayed it wouldn't be that merciless upholder of justice Pickles.

On the advice of my solicitor, David Adams, I changed tact and gave the obligatory 'no comment' throughout the interview; if I didn't say anything I couldn't make things any worse, if that was even possible. The judge might not look on it favourably further down the line but it was shit or bust, if I got seven years or ten years, what's the difference, really? It's still a decent stint, full stop.

They didn't need to, but the evidence was presented to me, so that I was under no illusion how close to the wall my back was. I'd been fingerprinted for the burglary at the Haulage Yard owner's home and eye-balled on both of the other two robberies, by whom I couldn't even begin to guess.

CLICK! The spring in Wilson's Parker twanged, the nib retracted and the interview concluded, procedures had been followed to the letter to ensure my conviction.

I was immediately placed on remand in the run up to my court hearing, to mull things over. The serious nature of the offences and the 'Old Bill's' certainty that they could convict me made sure of that. I was shipped out on remand the very next day to Thorp Arch over Tadcaster way, it was for Young Prisoners (YPs) only, I was still only nineteen years of age, but destined for mister's gaol sooner or later.

In some ways remand was a blessing, allowing you to chip away at whatever your inevitable fate may be, unless you're innocent, obviously, but that was rarely the case. I wasn't a flight risk, I knew that, but they didn't, another one of the reasons they'd put me on remand. I was a home bird, I loved Sheffield too much to skip off to the Costa del crime like my old pals Davy Dunford or Billy Barnes might have, that wasn't me. They didn't need to put me on remand, I wasn't going anywhere, the Wybourn life had clipped my wings long before now, but they couldn't take that chance. Like I said when you're bang to rights remand is a blessing, you're already chipping away at the inevitable, if you didn't view it that way you'd send yourself round the twist. No point kidding yourself you're being hard done to, that you're innocent, when you know you're not, even if I got off with the charges in court, I still owed society some form of debt.

I later found out they'd pulled the whole of our crew at the same time, the team from the Lyceum job, my lifelong pal Nicky Froggatt and the others, Tony Canetti, the getaway driver Mick Barker as well as my mentor Dave Lee, who'd orchestrated the Haulage Yard owner's burglary. A synchronised bust, we all lived in pretty much the same area of Sheffield, but the only connection to all three offences was me. This was real now, I was headed for mister's gaol, I was sure of that. I wouldn't see daylight after that for four years and ten months. How I had got to this point, one thing is for sure, it was my own doing, but let me explain....

FORGED IN SHEFFIELD

'Hillsborough, 1960'

I was born in Hillsborough, Sheffield on the 12th August 1960. People from other parts of the country might know the name of that place for another tragic reason, the disastrous events of April 15th 1989. Ninety-six innocent people lost their lives on the terraces of the Wednesday ground that day, not even Wednesday fans, but 'out of towners' who'd come to the area to watch the 1988–89 FA Cup semi-final between Liverpool and Notts Forest. Sheffield is renowned for many things, but that is not one we like to dwell upon, but also one that cannot be forgotten, god love those people, they are Hillsborough now.

I was brought up in Jordanthorpe, a lowly suburb of Sheffield, and a close knit breeding ground for the miner's and employees of the areas steel industry. A happy go lucky place of sorts, but one that bore the full brunt of the eventual economic downturn of both those industries.

I was the youngest of four siblings and like an excitable little puppy, the terror of the pack. The pack being made up of my two older brothers Peter and William, aka 'Our Billy', and my sister Ann. We were just another regular little Sheffield working class family. Pete was born in 1942 and my sister Ann five years later in 1947, both a fair bit older than me and both now with families of their own. Then along came my brother Billy, born in 1957. He was severely disabled but a character nonetheless, what he lacked in mobility he made up for in charisma. He was later to become the namesake for my own first born son, funnily enough called Billy, which was also my father's name, where Clyde came from who knows, I broke the mould in many ways.

I was raised on the Manor estate, a prefab, post war jungle, constructed after the war to house the labourers drawn into the area by Sheffield's ever growing Steel and Mining Industries. Everybody's old man or old dear was either directly or indirectly employed by those industries, unless you had a shop or ran the local pub, but who'd want those hassles on an estate like ours.

I was the son of the local 'coyl' man William Broughton, or 'Billy' as he was known by those who knew him. He was the stereotypical type, turning up home every night with a sooty face after a hard days slog. While my mum, his darling wife, Anne (maiden name Salvin) remained the archetypal housewife, making sure my old man was well looked after, after a hard day on the road lugging fifty kilo sacks around the local estates. These health and safety types wouldn't let you lift half of that these days, never mind the long hours he worked to ensure our extended family was taken care of.

My mother Anne was a housewife, just a few years younger than my old man, and they got on just fine, home life was good. She'd had my sister out of wedlock a few years before they'd met, so they put my mum in a workhouse, that's what they used to do back in those days, it sounds like something out of the history books now, but in reality it wasn't all that long ago really. It makes you realise how pointlessly brutal some of the 'old ways' were, I guess they had their reasons, restrictions to allow the system to work, but life could be harsh for people like my Mum.

Playing the woman of the house's role with four kids in tow, one of whom was severely disabled and another forever raising hell, her life can't have been easy. I bet just from chasing me around the house all day she'd have been as knackered as my dad was lugging coal sacks around the estate. Women were as big of a cog in the system as anyone else back then, it just wasn't acknowledged as such. That woman deserved medals, just like the ones my father earned in the war, but back then things were different.

My dad was born in 1914 and upon leaving school went straight into the army in 1939. York and Lance was his regiment. He was a Chindit. Fighting the 'Japs' in Burma, Africa, and Egypt etc.

Chindits were trained in Jungle Warfare. The largest of the allied Special Forces of the 2nd World War and operated deep behind enemy lines in North Burma in the war against Japan. For many months they lived in and fought the enemy in the jungles of Japanese occupied Burma, relying on airdrops for their supplies. To be a Chindit you had to be trained in guerrilla warfare. Their modus operandi, was to sneak up on their adversary and strangle them, dealing with their adversaries with their bare hands in the main.

My old man's best mate was a Gurka, another form of soldier. When they were holed up in hospital together after my Dad has been blown up he'd asked to see his pal the Gurka's sword. He was told by his friend that every time he drew the sword it HAD to draw blood so my old man ran his finger across the blade and cut it deep, it was so sharp it scarred him for life, but he deemed it worthwhile just to see the sword.

My Dad was a top man and had never been in trouble in his life, not one court appearance. There's a photo of him in his Chindit uniform, taking pride of place, hanging up in my bar to this day.

Early life was good, but never easy, but growing up in Sheffield was much the same for us all back in those days.

People didn't have much, but they didn't complain and they didn't really want for much anyway. You couldn't want for a nice motor or the latest mobile phone because those things just simply didn't exist back then, I guess if they didn't now crime rates would be much lower, somebody always wants what you've got, and they don't always want to work to get it. I was for a long time one of those people.

Growing up I was never far from trouble, it had to be something in my genes, I have no excuses, I was always criminally inclined and it certainly wasn't the fault of my parents. Like I said, my old man never had a court appearance in his life, something which filled him with pride.

As it turns out I needed a little more to occupy my mind than most of the kids on the estate and that's where things really started to go wrong. My natural inclination towards sports and the need for an athletic output probably also played a factor. They might call it ADHD these days, but that was nonsense, I was simply a 'wrong-un'. My requirement to outrun the law as a way of burning off that excess energy always prevailed, there were never any medals on offer, just cold hard time. Well so be it, I had to run and run I did.

I started to really go off the rails when I was only about ten years old, a scrawny little thing with fluffy blonde hair, would you believe. I know that sounds young, and to be honest it was. It was only general thieving here and there to begin with, and mostly for fun, not financial again. Consequences didn't register with me back then, in fact they just didn't matter. I always had to take things one step further. Luckily for me I had a number of wayward pals who were happy to join me in my endeavours, but one who has been by my side throughout is Nicky Froggatt. He was my best mate from school, and still to this day, nearly fifty years on. He's done a couple of five stretches himself, one was in Wakefield, and I can honestly say he is, sorry was, categorically the best Shoplifter I've ever met.

Being naturally athletic, my speed gave me the upper hand over the local 'bobbies' or anyone else who happened to be on my case. I was fast, I might have landed up in trouble many more times in my life if it wasn't for my natural agility and speed, but nine times out of ten no one could catch me, certainly not the fat old plods that patrolled our blessed Jordanthorpe. But let's not forget, the tortoise always eventually beats the hair, I'd outrun the local shopkeeper and then a nosey neighbour would clock me and ring the police, they'd always eventually turn up at my parents door, you know how it goes.

My dear old Mum would often send me to the nearby Co-op shop, the local Newsagents and Grocers rolled into one, with a bag for food, necessities such as a loaf of bread or a tin of beans with a few shilling. I'd put what I'd been sent for (and sometimes a few luxuries) in the bag and pocket the money, everybody was happy, apart from the shopkeeper though I'm not sure my mum would have been if she'd known.

When I got to around twelve years old that's when I started to get more serious about my criminal activities elevating to smaller burglaries such as schools, stealing motorbikes, I couldn't even ride them, I was always the Pillion. I still can't ride a bike to this day, never mind at twelve, but we took them anyway, me and my good pal Froggatt.

It was only a matter of time before I ended up in approved school or Borstal, my first stint came when I was just twelve years old.

DREAMS OF NAUGHTINESS

'1972 onwards…'

I was twelve years old the first time I got sent away. Sent off to an assessment centre / care home in Sheffield called Shirecliffe. I remember that day like it was yesterday. A council representative from the 'naughty boys' squad turned up at our house with a folder firmly tucked under his arm that had my name emblazoned across the front.

I'd sensed it coming, but to my poor parents it came as somewhat of a shock. These days you'd probably receive a thousand letters and numerous visits before being carted away at an age like that, but this was 1972 and things were a little different.

After the pleading from my parents had fallen on deaf ears, I was whisked away to a care home in Sheffield, under the guise it was the best thing for me. The care home was to be merely a halfway house to my ultimate destination of Borstal.

Prior to being sent to Borstal I was made to attend Juvenile Court where they sent me away for three weeks for an assessment at Shirecliffe whilst under a care order. It was my first taste of harsh reality, but it would take more than that to faze me.

Shirecliffe was brutal and it wasn't uncommon to receive 'six of the best' for stepping out of line, right there in the main hall in front of everyone, but you didn't cry, that was your only remaining dignity, but 'by Christ' you wanted to. Thankfully the place has been demolished now, but further down the line there were many claims of much more serious abuse in the remand homes, claims of physical, mental degradation and worse. Those places ruined many lives and affected people for years to come, but not mine.

I read an article in The Sheffield Star many years ago about claims of kids suffering physical and mental degradation during their time at Shirecliffe. If you didn't do your jobs right you were cracked. I have to be honest and say I don't remember any of that, or indeed the short stints I did there ever fazing me, but I have no doubt such things went off. If I got the slipper for being out of line, or whatever, I don't class that as physical abuse, maybe some would. It was a harsh place, but life was like that at that time and I do not feel I was treat in a way that scarred me in later life. Though I feel for those that it did. I can honestly say these things never happened to me, I'm not saying they didn't to others, I'm sure they did, but I'd made it through unscathed, unaffected, ready to take on the world, one crime at a time, sometimes more.

I temporarily returned home, but the trouble persisted. My parents had pleaded for me to come home and it was granted, but within just a few weeks I was sent back again for wagging school.

Eventually I was put under a care order up until the age of fifteen, which meant I had to attend approved school for three years at Castle Howard in Malton, North Yorkshire or as it was previously and rather cumbersomely called 'The Society for the Reformation of Juvenile Offenders for the East and North Ridings of the County of York and the Town and County of Kingston upon Hull', a title which would later prove very handy for achieving my story's word count.

I would like to say that, hand on heart, all this was no real reflection on my parents, it's just how I was, my unwillingness to conform just seemed to be something I was born with and has continued right to this day. In all honesty the care order was the best thing for me, going off the rails. Mum and Dad also knew deep down it was the best place for me, wagging school and burglaries, things were now going too far. My parents had no control, I just did what I wanted. Though despite all that they were devastated that I was away from home. I was still the baby of the household in some respects and I regret that I upset them in that way to this very day.

Forget what you've heard, to me it (Castle Howard) was like a holiday camp really. I absconded a few times and tried to make my way home. Just twelve years old and out at two o'clock in the morning, pitch black, ploughing through fields, trying to get home. Eventually after going round in circles for hours on end, I'd be done in and head back to the approved school, I'd tried, that's what counted.

I had a few like-minded friends that I hooked up with there, ones with the same wayward tendencies and the desire to make their way back home and have a bit of fun along the way. Ones like Kevin Bottomley from Mytholmroyd near Todmorden, Ronnie Spencer from Hull and the now infamous Ronnie Pickering from Kingston upon Hull, you know who he is right? He was a sound kid back then, I'd also meet up with him later again in Borstal.

Whenever we absconded from Castle Howard it was always the same faces tagging along, me Kevin and the two Ronnies from Hull, all lads form the same house.

One particular night we'd all absconded. Our aim was to get over to Kevin's neck of the woods in Mytholmroyd about fifteen miles away. Some task on foot, and even more so in the dark.

We weren't going to last very long without a stitch to our name, just the clothes on our back, so we broke into an old terraced house not too far from the reform school and had found around £300 in cash, which was a considerable sum back then for a bunch of young hoodlums.

We'd made it about thirteen miles from York and to our destination, how we got to Mytholmroyd in the dark I have no idea. We went in to Todmorden town centre and all bought brand new clothes, the likes of which we would never normally be able to afford, Mytholmroyd instantly becoming the Milan of West Yorkshire.

"How come you've got all this money lads?" The shop owner enquired.

"We save up and come out once a year to spend it" We fannied him with a smirk.

He knew it was bollocks, he'd be on the phone to the old bill before the shop door had even clasped shut.

Half an hour later we were sat about on some old climbing frames nearby, whiling away the hours, when the coppers turned up. We didn't even run, we were bang to rights and we knew all they would do was ship us straight back to the reform school.

At the time 'Spud' Tate was our house master, by coincidence he also played for Sheffield Wednesday, but I was getting no favours for my local association and he made sure we were duly punished.

He'd made us put on these decrepit old hobnail boots, the traditional type with leather laces, then tied all three of us together, we sure as hell weren't going anywhere now. They were so uncomfortable, you couldn't have made it more than fifty yards with those on and we'd had to sleep that way too.

A short time after our little group was split up and I never really saw any of those lads again, apart from Ronnie Pickering who I met again later whilst at Borstal.

I stayed in that place until age fifteen when I was finally allowed home.

I eventually did two Detention Centres (Wetherby and Watton), for worse thieving, mostly burgling houses. We'd shifted the gear we stole, using local contacts, mostly by hanging out around the outside of the busier pubs. As we got older we got into other things. There were a few pins, faces with real money, from the local area who we took things to first, but it all had to go. But my crimes hadn't gone unnoticed, hence the reason I ended up in Borstal.

One of my favourite places was Wetherby. There were plenty of sports on offer as well as getting my two weekly visits from my bird at the time. I was happy there, I had no need to flee.

When you went for your induction at Wetherby you had to run a quarter of Wetherby Race Course, this was to get a measure of who was capable of what, but also a small form of punishment for the lazier amongst the group. The course record was twenty five minutes. My first attempt I made it round in twenty three minutes. I was a good all rounder when it came to sports, whether it be football, basketball or even trampolining and it wasn't long before it was being noticed. The house masters were always on my case because I was a flash cunt, as in they made me do the quarter of the racecourse again, straight away, but this time I had to jump the fences like an old nag, basically because they didn't like the fact I'd broken the record and now they wanted to break me, but I did it, I cut myself to shreds but I did it.

The screws didn't like me, but they didn't like me even more once I'd done it a second time, though eventually they grew to love me because I excelled at sports and they made me up to an Orderly, it also helped as it was the same screw from Watton, who knew me.

I was in Watton Detention Centre, near Nottingham twice, also a young offender. It was there that I encountered other like-minded individuals, or rogues. I was supposedly there for rehabilitation, but us 'wrong-uns' bounced off each other, harvesting ideas, sharing useful techniques, growing in criminal confidence, if anything the punishment was counterproductive.

'OUR BILLY'

'Patch's Primeval Sob'

Billy my brother was diagnosed as severely disabled from about the age of six, spending the most part of his life in a wheelchair. Though he still had is faculties with him, for the best part, his condition grew gradually worse as each year passed and more rapidly, by the day, towards the very end of his life.

I dare say if he had been born in current times the resources and know-how available would have given him a much better standard of life and he may have lived to a much riper age, but this was the 1960's and life wasn't what it is now.

I loved my brother Billy dearly, and will always remember the times we spent together, no matter how restricted and usually in the confines of our shared bedroom when I was on leave from approved school. We made the most of that space, with only our imaginations and a few old books and comics to occupy ourselves there was never a dull moment. I still remember those times fondly.

I've had only a few regrets in my life but maybe the time I spent away from home back then, for my unruly behaviour, had lessened the amount of time I got to spend with him during his short life, if I do have a regret somewhere in me that is it.

Regarding his condition and to be blunt, he were 'fucked from the off'. He couldn't feed himself, or even turn himself over in bed at night. Imagine what that must be like, the types of things that me and you take for granted. He'd have to shout my Dad to come and help him, just to turn over in bed at night. His brittle bones meant he could do little more, all the things that me and you don't even have to think about were beyond his reach.

I was only fourteen when he died. I was in the bedroom with him when it happened. It shook me to my core, but I would never say that it was the catalyst for my 'bad behaviour.' I was already naughty well before that, I could never use his death as a reason for me to go off the rails. That would be disrespectful to his memory and in all honesty a load of bollocks.

I remember him dying and the few days that led up to it. Every now and then I'd be allowed home for the weekend. Though I enjoyed that time it didn't deter me from playing up, but on those rare occasions I was home I shared a bedroom with my brother Billy.

Though physically restricted his mental faculties were all there, in fact he was a lot sharper than some of the idiots I was at Borstal with, that was for sure. He was sound of mind, a clever kid really, and he never complained, some testament to his character, the one that lied beneath the brittle bones, a wonderful mind.

On those rare occasions I got weekend release from Castle Howard, my Mum and Dad were always pleased to see me. They often pleaded with the approved School to let me come back home for good, or at least more often, but it wasn't going to happen. It didn't matter how bad things got or how much trouble I brought to their door, they loved me and my siblings unconditionally.

I, more than any of them, must have really tested their resolve, taking advantage of their good nature in some respects, not something I'm proud of, possibly another one of my few regrets.

It was on one of those fleeting visits home that it happened, something that has haunted me for the rest of my days. Though away from home more often than not I still shared a room with my brother Billy and I loved him dearly, he could always put a smile on my face.

I regretted being away from home so much. Sharing a room made us close, especially since my brother couldn't leave it, I guess to him those times were more precious than for me, being stuck in there, the company a small form of escape. We'd sit around and I'd tell him what I'd been up to, read him whatever he asked for, grab him something to eat, it was never a chore for me to help our Billy.

We'd chat, read books, do whatever we could within the boundaries of his restrictions, even in the confines of our bedroom we made our own entertainment and me and our Billy were happy.

As time wore on, I could see his condition deteriorating and becoming gradually worse, only a young lad by any ones standards, but no real quality of physical life, but his mental side was all there, brighter than some of the drips on the Manor estate.

These days he could barely do anything for himself. It had gotten so bad my Dad had to come out of work to care for him. His condition was serious, more serious than I could understand only being young myself. My Dad must have been shattered, turning him over two or three times a night, my Dad must have gone through the mill himself, they never once gave up on him.

I'd just come home on one of my not so frequent bursts of leave from Castle Howard, I'd only just walked into the bedroom when I realised things were not right, but Dad had already raised the alarm and moments later the room was full of noise and commotion. Our beloved pet dog Patch instinctively knew something was wrong, laid at the side of our Billy's bed howling his own primeval sob.

Ambulance men, Doctors marched through, I was no expert but I knew the time had come, they tried frantically to find some hope, but they knew, even more so than me, it as a wasted effort.

That day is forever etched in my mind, what life had my brother had? Mine so eventful and blazing, maybe I'd received both our share of athleticism and fire, in any event it wasn't fair, he didn't deserve that, but then so often life isn't.

Though home on compassionate grounds I didn't attend our Billy's funeral. My parents thought it might be too much for me at my age, and me and Billy being so close, but I never went back when this happened, I was fourteen years old and absconded for the final time, in some respects the authorities had given up on me, but I hadn't given up on myself.

My Mother later told me they had given him up to 21, he died when he was just 18, a testament to the pain he must have gone through, god bless his soul. They kept that from me, for the best I think, and I'd have to agree.

Years later and in honour of my brother we named our first son Billy. A constant reminder of my brother, whom I wish was still here today, but praise the lord that his ailments were finally cured and he was taken to a better place. God Bless our Billy!

TRIALS AT WEDNESDAY

'Big Jack'

As you'll soon read, I've attended plenty of trials over the years, but they weren't all of the criminal type. I've always been naturally athletic, and was easily good enough to play football professionally, but I just didn't have the commitment or concentration span for it. I'm sure there's many promising young lads out there who 'never quite made it' for various reasons and I was one of them and my reason was I preferred to misbehave.

My first real love in life had always been football, not criminality. That was just my way of life, a means to an end. I'd be lying if I said I didn't get some thrill from outfoxing the law, but I didn't get the great joy from it that I did with football. I'm part of the history of Burton Albion, I was with them for eighteen months, before they got into the league, when they were in the Multipart's League and Brian Fiddler was the manager. I've also played for the two oldest clubs in the world, which are Sheffield FC and Hallam FC, back when they were in the North East Counties.

Whilst I was in Borstal at Wetherby and playing regularly for the in-house team one of the teachers, unbeknown to me, had contacted Sheffield Wednesday and asked them to come and scout me.

A week or so later, a scout by the name of John Harris attended one of my matches whilst playing for the Borstal team, and immediately requested my presence at

Wednesday's ground the following week to showcase my skills in front of the, then, manager Jack Charlton, or 'Big Jack' as he was known.

Jack Charlton Managed Sheffield Wednesday from the 8th October 1977 to 27 May 1983. During that period Wednesday played 269 matches, won 105, lost 77 and drew 8. Big Jack's time at Hillsborough is revered by Owls fans, even to this day. In the doldrums in the Old Division Three, he was appointed as manager in October 1977.

With the Owls struggling he managed to stabilise the club in his first two seasons and they finished 14th two years running. But what he gave the club was a heartbeat, a focus, a passion. He was a high profile manager and with that came expectation. I couldn't have been asked to showcase my skills in front of a more qualified man.

In the 1979-80 season he also gave Wednesday supporters a moment in their history they will always remember, 'The Thrashing', you know the one, the Boxing Day Massacre. Stuffing our dark cousins from across the city and forever to be written in Sheffield folklore. With United top of the table and Wednesday in 4th place it was supposed to be a walkover for the Blades, but things didn't quite go to plan, it could be argued the result changed the fortunes of both clubs. For that one game alone Big Jack is a hero to Wednesday fans.

To cap off the season, for the first time in five years the Owls also got promoted, finishing 3rd in the league with the Blades never recovering from that hiding and going on to be relegated to the bottom tier the season after. What an impact Big Jack had.

And this Legend was the manager at the time I'd been selected for trials, the guy who came and scouted me went by the name of John Harris. He'd only watched me play seriously a couple of times, we'd sometimes play outside teams, straight teams, not other naughty boys. In fact we were actually in a local league when he agreed that I should come down for trials.

I went for trials, I think I was playing for the under 17's at that time, who were having a little friendly against the men's reserves team. Like a duck to water, I scored two goals. In fact Jack Charlton was actually playing just behind me in mid-field, as part of the friendly / training, showing the lads how it was done.

This was at the Middlewood road ground, a real football ground / training facility. At that time, I was a lot different to the other lads there, I was a rogue; I didn't fit in, if that makes sense. I'd turned up with my football boots and shinnies in a carrier bag, whilst everyone else was nicely turned out with their clean new Adidas sports bags. I usually played on the right wing, but often played in the centre when instructed. My pace was my real asset; no one and I mean no one could catch me once I was off. I wasn't the most skilful player or the best in the air, I might only get two goals a season with my head, but give me a yard of space and if I turned around they were in trouble. I was known for my pace. I don't think the others knew I was from Borstal, but I felt like a fish out of water around these people, the way they carried themselves, the way they spoke.

I nervously laced up my boots in the changing rooms, I didn't know a soul in that room, in fact I don't think I spoke to anyone the whole two hours I was there. My heart was racing as I followed the other lads down the tunnel and on to the pitch. I stared around in amazement, this was of a scale bigger than anything I'd ever played on. I genuinely felt the anticipation of an FA Cup final in my bones.

We did a few warm up exercises under Big Jack's instruction, all standard stuff. I didn't need to warm up, I needed that ball at my feet. After a bit of one-two it was time to play for real.

I headed straight for my natural wing position, no one had directed me, if I was the first there, they'd know I had the confidence of my role and who from this lot of mummy's boys was going to tell me otherwise.

The whistle went, there was a bit of pointless preamble, the kind you see in most football matches, each side weighing their opponents up, even becoming accustomed to their own teammates, this bunch were cobbled together, like I said I didn't know a soul, I wasn't going to just give the ball away easily to the guy to my right, what if he wasn't up to standard? What if he was better than me? I didn't want to give him the opportunity to shine brighter than me.

A good ten minutes in and the ball arrived at my feet. I was mid-way into the other teams half and knew I had the pace to run rings around half of these fools. I tapped the ball to the left of their midfielder, chased it down, ran it another ten yards or so and BANG! It came off my left foot like a rocket, I could hit the ball with either. It whistled past the keepers reach and lodged itself firmly in the top corner of the net, ten minutes in and old Jack was already seeing what young Clyde was all about.

The game meandered on for another sixty minutes or so before my next moment to shine. We'd quickly progressed down the field when the kid to my left, a lanky ginger kid put in a near perfect ball to my head, I merely had to nod and it was going past the bemused goalie. It ricocheted off my head, down to the floor and back up into the net. It took close to zero effort, but it made me look the outstanding man of the trials, whoever that kid was I owed him a pint, or two.

Come the end of the ninety minute practise / friendly I was relieved that it was over, our side had won, I had been integral in the outcome, it couldn't have gone any better. I could have played another half hour if needs be, but in truth the sooner that whistle blew the better I looked, less time for the tide to turn, our side to lose and my efforts pale into the fore.

I knew the trial had gone well, not just the two goals. I hadn't let the pressure get to me and played as if it were a local home game. Still, from the unease I felt around these people, I just thought fuck it I can't cope with this shit. After the game, I picked my bag up and walked out.

John Harris, the scout, knew something wasn't right, he knew what was going through my head. He came over to me and said "Clyde what are you doing?" He looked genuinely upset for me.

"It's not for me," I made my excuses and turned my back. Then I said "I'm off, I didn't play very well." I knew I had, but I just wanted out of there.

"Well you must have done summat reyt, because he (Jack Charlton) wants to see you again TOMORROW!" He continued.

Anyway, I promised him that I'd be back the next day, but I knew it wasn't for me and I never returned... Big mistake.

CRIME APPRENTICESHIP

'RIP Dave Lee'

The turning point for me into serious criminality came not long after I'd gotten out of Borstal, aged just eighteen. That little break from the outside world had given me all the respite I needed to get back into the fold of criminality on the streets of Sheffield.

I'd just come out of a Detention Centre in Watton, Nottingham. No 'real' rehabilitation had taken place, I still had the same zest for life and criminality I'd had before I'd been sent there, and I'd made a few friends along the way.

Just like every other time I'd been on the out, the first thing I did was find myself a local football team to 'sign-on' with and do what I loved doing most, playing football. I never stayed with many teams long, as I was always in and out of the nick. But whenever I was out I always got straight back into the team. Everyone wanted 'Broughts' on their squad in our area. I'd have played football all day everyday back then, perhaps if I'd taken my trials at Wednesday more seriously my life could have taken a different path. Under the trusty wing of Big Jack my skills could have flourished, but I'd chosen the alternative and was relishing any opportunity I could to make a few quid and have a good time.

I'd started playing for one of the better local teams, Darnall Green FC which was run out of their working men's club house. Then I 'signed' for the Springwood another local boozer and eventually moved on to

Arbourthron East Avenue (EA), the best team in our area. Though it was my time at Darnall Green FC that would prove to be the most significant and ultimately shape the direction of my life, it was there that I first ran into the infamous Dave Lee, one of Sheffield's most notorious crooks.

At that time Darnall Green FC was being run out of their club house, funnily enough in Darnall, a place I would eventually grow to call my second home, especially now I was old enough to drink on licensed premises. I'd had no real trouble getting in the squad after displaying my skills in one of their mid-week training sessions.

By pure coincidence the team was being run at that time by one of Sheffield's most notorious faces, a man by the name of Dave Lee. I already knew of him and a little of what he was about, and it wouldn't be long before I was firmly tucked under his wing and we were 'grafting' together, that's a term we use for criminal work.

Dave Lee was infamous in Sheffield, though maybe not known too well to the wider world, apart from in the criminal fraternity or the gaol house. But in the circles I wanted to move in he was the most notorious crook in our area. If I couldn't line my pockets working with him then I may as well pack it in and go get a job down the pit, become a wagon driver or something equally as mundane.

Dave Lee was a hard man from the Woodthorpe area of Sheffield and well known for villainy. He wasn't one to fuck about with, he would take on anyone, win or lose. A villain, and a real one at that, a fair bit older than me, well established and ready to guide me in the ways of criminality. A big, menacing, good looking cunt and strong as an Ox. A similar size to Paul Sykes and a good footballer to boot.

He'd done a nine stretch, and a ten, that's where he'd met Sykesy, the Lambrianou brothers, and a few other faces from the British underworld. I knew he was a good pal of the Boxer Paul Sykes, another notorious character in Yorkshire crime circles, a professional heavyweight and someone I was to hook up with further down the line. He was a man notorious for his lack of social boundaries and hilarious antics, but also not someone to mess with.

Dave Lee bowed to no one. I'd even heard he'd once had a bit of a bust up with Tony Lambrianou in Hull Nick. They'd eventually ended up across the room from each other slinging salt and pepper pots at each other. Sykesy was the one who told me about that, by the way, it had to be true, you couldn't make that kind a scenario like that up.

He'd also once robbed the Strines pub on the outskirts of Sheffield. The police were on his trail and he'd had to live rough on the Moors for several days. I believe he was considered the most wanted / dangerous man in the country at that particular time. They didn't have police helicopters back then so he took some finding, but they did find him eventually.

Sometime later he got a nine stretch for drugs, the details of which I never really knew. He was sent down along with another mate of mine, Steve Bagley, who'd been given 'a six'. I wasn't involved in that one, thank god. Though my turn would eventually come.

Dave Lee has passed away now, god rest his soul, but he was a hard bastard in his time. Not quite Paul Sykes' level, don't get me wrong, but a feared and somewhat respected man in Sheffield and well known all over the country in criminal quarters.

Anyway we'd become good friends through our local football team Darnall Green FC, through our mutual passion, still one of mine to this day. There were a few villains on that squad, let me tell you. I think at some point our paths must have been destined to cross, he was aware of my background and I was aware of his standing. You often see people around your home town who intrigue you and sooner or later you find a way to initiate a conversation, you know without knowing that you're gonna 'get on', work together maybe. Some of the best friendships, business partnerships and disastrous outcomes have come about that way, it always goes either one way or the other. Sheffield might have a population of over five hundred thousand, but it was only a matter of time before me and Dave Lee hooked up.

Dave instantly latched on to my footballing skills and my addiction to making a fast quid. Within a matter of weeks of me turning up at Darnall, I was involved in various criminal errands and up to my neck in burglaries with him. Before long I'd graduated to more serious robberies, often with Dave or based upon one of his, usually accurate / well informed, tip-offs. Whether we'd gone together or me on my own either way he was getting his cut. We worked together on many occasions, it worked well, until the wheels eventually fell off - they usually do at some point when you're in that deep.

Through association with Dave Lee, things quickly moved to the next level for me. I had no trade behind me as such, like so many in Sheffield at that time, nor any inclination to wade into the steel business that kept our city ticking over. I had to graft in the only way I knew. I'm not making out I had some terrible start in life that sent me down the wrong path, I make no bones about it, I loved every minute. It wasn't ideal and certainly nothing to be proud of, but that's my life and that's where it went.

We wasted no time when it came to grafting and making money, and we kept our circle tight, all the principles and tricks Dave had picked up in his years of criminality were passed on to me. I'd cut through half the mistakes he'd made and gone straight to graduation, after a somewhat brief apprenticeship. He used me in a way when we'd first met; he couldn't fit through windows and I could, simple as that.

Wherever possible we kept our business to ourselves and ran a very small crew, in fact often just me and Dave. Why bring someone in whose capabilities might not see the job through? If you did it yourself the job was getting done and it was getting done right, there was nowhere else to point the finger when things went wrong. We had some good wages, week in week out. Things were running smoothly in our little criminal quarter.

When we'd started I was still somewhat of a nervous young kid and it took time to develop my metal. In one more memorable incident I'd once burgled a house in one of the more upmarket areas of town. Dave had dropped me off around the corner.

"Don't be alarmed Clyde, but the doors in the house are all belled up" He said, meaning if you opened one they were wired up and a bell would ring within the house. Which didn't matter 'two fucks' if no one was in.

"But don't worry the place is empty" Don't worry?! I was only about eighteen and frightened to death.

I went in through the living room window and froze, I didn't dare go any further. I took everything I could of value from that one room. The stress of the situation was really starting to get to me, and before I left I took a shit on the carpet! Not really something to be proud of and if I'm honest it wasn't an act of defiance, it actually came down to nerves, not bravado. I made out I was the funny man after I'd left, but in truth the nerves had gotten the better of me. I'd learnt a valuable lesson there, make sure you've been to the toilet before you set off on any journey, especially a burglary.

Dave started to introduce me to all manner of people, just like JP Bean's book 'Gang Wars of Sheffield', the names and faces of Sheffield's criminal world still existed: Dave Lee, Freddie Bonzo, David Dunford. Dunford was a proper villain who'd worked with the likes of Ronnie Knight and a few more of the 'more glamorous' out of town crooks. He was one of the main men for the importation of cannabis into the UK from Spain back in the day, so he was rolling in cash back then. I'm sure he wouldn't mind me telling you because he's served his time, getting on now and completely retired from the game. He was also the one that had told me that Sykesy had knocked Roy Shaw out twice whilst in Hull Nick. He'd also been shot himself whilst out in Spain, that man has led some life.

I'd first met Davy Dunford at the Springwood when I was sixteen, he was there with Paul Sykes and a few other known villains. There were always the same names and faces hanging about the Springwood, Freddie Bonzo aka Fat Freddie was another. He wasn't a villain as such, but he was in with the Prices, working with scrap, buying and selling horses, by no means a serious criminal but definitely an enabler and often in criminal company.

Dave introduced me to a few other faces from the North's criminal fraternity, some local and some from further afield, such as Paul Sykes from Wakefield, Delroy Showers from Liverpool 8, Billy Barnes from Leeds and a few others from over Manchester way. Types he'd most likely hooked up with whilst in the nick and then continued his friendship of convenience with on the outside.

I remember the first time I met Paul Sykes like it was yesterday, this was way before any real criminal associations I would make with him. Me and a few of my pals were sat in the Springwood, like we usually would. Always the liveliest pub on the Manor / Woodthorpe area, the place always had somewhat of a bad reputation but it was one we'd happily frequent. Those places never fazed us, when you're from the area they're not so daunting. The Springwood is closed now, long gone, but those boozers gave the Manor character and defined those times.

Anyway Paul had come over to the Springwood with David Dunford or Davy, as Paul referred to him in his book 'Sweet Agony'. I was sat in the Springwood with my pals, only about sixteen or seventeen years old at the time, considerably younger than Paul and his associates.

They walked in, Paul the man-mountain, Davy Dunford, Dave Lee and a black guy by the name of Delroy Showers from Liverpool. Anyway this not so little team had come over because Davy Dunford had been getting some hassle from a local guy, none other than Freddie Bonzo. Davy wasn't really a fighter and Freddie was a big bloke, hence the reason Paul was in tow. They turned up in a big black Rolls Royce, owned by Delroy Showers, a major pin from Liverpool but a real nice guy.

Needless to say word had spread and Freddie Bonzo never showed, but I'd been introduced to Paul and our friendship was cemented for further down the line when we reconvened in prison.

As Freddie Bonzo hadn't shown, Delroy did the honourable thing and took all the local kids hanging around outside the pub for a ride in his black Rolls Royce. He also gave them all a tenner a piece out of kindness. Remember, this was circa. 1977 and that was a lot of money back then. Seriously, I wish I'd have gotten in that Roller and held my hand out for a tenner, instead of grafting for it.

The second time I met Sykesy he'd come back to the Springwood again. Because I was grafting with Dave at the time I was sat within their group now. Somewhat awe struck, I remember Paul was fast becoming a name in professional boxing. I remember the first thing I ever said to him like it was yesterday.

"Paul, will you have your picture took with me missus?" Guess what he came back with?

"Only if I can I put my fingers up her fanny?" Remember I told you about his lack of social boundaries.

I'm fucking dead serious, and I was only about seventeen years old. Stopped in my tracks by a giant of a guy in his early thirties who was as good as local mafia. I didn't know whether to laugh or cry, anyway, it was all taken in jest, we continued to have a few drinks and from then on I classed Paul as a friend.

I'll never forget him and the times we had, many a time I would go to his house over in Wakefield, but it would always lead somewhere further afield. Life was never straight forward where Sykesy was concerned.

I remember one occasion Dave Lee he had a go at the man mountain himself. Dave was fearless, but that particular incident didn't really go his way.

One particular day we were in Dave's old car. Dave was driving the Volvo, Cath (Paul's missus) was in the front and me, Sykesy and Sue Lee (Dave's missus) were in the back. We were hurtling down the M1 and Sykesy was trying to get a kiss off Sue and she elbowed him away, so he clipped her, not hard enough to do damage but hard enough for it to be deemed disrespectful. Dave saw red, slammed the anchors on and swerved over on to the hard shoulder. He dragged his missus out to get to Sykesy and said "Come on Sykesy, get the fuck out!"

Sue was saying to me, "Clyde, do something!," And I'm thinking, what the fuck am I gonna do with these two big lumps? So I got out and tried to calm the situation down.

"Come on lads, calm it down." I said, but it was too late.

I looked over at Sykesy and he was in a textbook Boxing defensive position, rocking about, or weaving as it is called in their game.

"A' waint hit ye Dave, I'll oni block thi." Mocking Dave's abilities and re-emphasising his own.

Luckily things diffused from there. Dave Lee would have had a go mind, but no one could take Sykesy on. He knew how to fight, not just box. He could fight dirty, you never saw that on camera, never mind the boxing, he was fucking ruthless. I've seen photos of him with Larry Holmes, you don't get to spar with people like that if you're a mug.

These were only fleeting brushes with some notorious characters, but I was young and I'd been noticed and that would be enough to help me out if I ended up in gaol and it wasn't long before that's where I ended up.

A NICE LITTLE WIN AT THE BOOKIES

'Alison Crescent'

Most days of the week I could be found down the Springwood on Hastilar Road, on the Manor. That place was always one of my regular haunts and one of my favourite pubs right up until its closure a few years back. Many a plan had been hatched in there, some I'd live to regret but many that helped me live the lifestyle I was becoming accustomed to.

I'd often be down there early in the afternoon having a few pints with my pals, usually lads from the pub football team, for whom I was a regular player when I wasn't banged up.

I'd always have a bit of banter with the owner Mick, sometimes wind up a few or the more straight laced regulars, but there was never any malice and it was always in good jest.

Everyone knew everyone in there back then, maybe not by their full, or even their real name, but nicknames or whatever, the fine details were never important at that age, you knew who was worth knowing and who wasn't, who was an arsehole and who would help you out when it came down to it.

It became my office of sorts. I was never a big drinker back in those days. I could easily spend half a day down there and sip away at only two pints, maybe three if forced. There was often a little bit of business to be done and many of my activities meant I needed my wits about me, and that doesn't happen when you're half-cut.

I was still playing football for the Springwood at the time, alongside my mentor Dave Lee, even more of a reason to be down there. It was an ideal place to hatch our plans.

It was just another one of those days. I was down there with my usual pint of whatever happened to be on tap that month and chatting to some of my pals about football, boxing, I birds and any little scams that were up for grabs.

RING! RING! The pub's pay phone at the side of the bar rang. These were the days before the arrival of the mobile phone and if it rang the chances were it could be for any of us sat in that place. Usually one of your pals checking if you were down there before setting off or your missus giving you a bollocking because the tea was burnt and was about to be fed to the hound. On the odd occasion it was for the Landlord; the brewery letting him know a delivery was imminent or another local landlord tipping them off about rowdy punters or an impending visit from the Bobbies for after hours.

RING! RING! The pub pay phone went again, like it did every half hour or so, but this time it appeared to be about to rattle right off its mechanism, that inanimate object somehow knowing this particular call was important.

The landlord Mick grabbed it with a look on his face that said something along the lines of 'Who the fuck is ringing at this time of day' Like he always did, regardless of the time.

A couple of seconds passed. He spun around and shouted over, "Clyde it's for you." His tone no different from any other time it had happened.

I casually wandered over and took the receiver from him, "Hello?" I asked inquisitively.

"Clyde, listen," The voice came back.

No introduction was required. I recognised that voice instantly, it was my old pal Rodney Fisher. If he was ringing me on the Springwood hotline then there was something interesting afoot, usually a tip for a nag that was quickly making its way in to favourite or the offer of some knocked off goods.

He continued "There's a lad heading back from the bookies... down the Prince of Wales Road" I knew exactly where he meant.

"He'll be hitting Alison Crescent any minute," I had an inkling what was coming next.

"He's just had a stroke of luck... twelve hundred quid. I don't know what he's got on him, but it's yours." He sniggered, in a manner that said you owe me a drink for this one! Not literally, it would be a ton minimum, though the job needed sorting first, I could think about that later.

"I'm on it," I replied and the receiver went down before he had chance to respond or I could make thanks. There was no point letting the ear-wiggers hear anything more than was necessary.

I'd already made my mind up without really assessing what I was about to take on; I was the bookies lucky punter now. I put my pint down and mumbled a bit of something for effect, words but not words, not that anyone was really listening, something along the lines of, 'Just nipping out for a fag'.

I calmly walked towards the beer garden door, and the second I was outside, even before the door had closed behind me, I was off like an XR3i - nought to sixty in literally no time at all.

I had no idea what I was letting myself in for, it could have been the hardest bloke on the estate or an off duty copper for all I knew; naïve really, but I'd committed and there was no way I'd back out now, even if he had the local rugby team in tow.

I continued to leg it down Hastilar Road in the direction of Alison Crescent with the dogged determination of a man on a promise. I knew the route well but I'd be taking a different one back to the Springwood that was for sure. There was no way I could miss the kid with the speed at which I'd reacted to the call, with my lack of delay I knew I'd reach the junction he had to cross at near as damn it the same time as he would.

I clocked him. Rodney had briefly described the guy: 'Brown Bag, Black Coat, 'headin' for the bottom of Alison Crescent', that was enough for me and if I was wrong then someone else was getting it. I can't emphasize how important the supply of information was back then, but I have to be honest and say in this case I hadn't taken the time I should have to make sure things went to plan.

I dropped my pace and slowed to what could only be described as a bizarre, but fast, walk, giving the appearance I was about to miss out on a dead cert. in the next race at Kempton myself.

As I came close to the guy, I perched on my toes and launched a right hook straight into his face, his nose made a sound like it had shattered, a noise like a bottle being thrown at a wall. I'd only meant to stun him enough to take the winnings, but I'd inadvertently done him a real injustice. He hit the floor like he'd never get back up, not giving him enough time to clearly eyeball me.

I grabbed him by the collar, while he was still out cold. After rifling through his pockets I relieved him of his winnings, if I'd left it now then I really would have been a fool, I'd gone too far not to make it worth the while. I had no real time to count it, but I'd seen a grand or two before and I knew he didn't have anything like twelve hundred quid on him. Then it dawned on me... the local bookies would never dish out that kind of cash in a 'oner' on our estate, they'd be lucky to have that kind of money in the till at all. As it turned out he didn't have the whole £1,200 on him. They'd given him £800 and an 'IOU' for the remaining £400 as they didn't have that much in the shop or at least they'd have had to shut shop for the rest of the day without their float. I even had the ticket mingled in with the pile of cash, I could, with the right sized bollocks, wonder into another branch and try and get my hands on the rest. Not likely, I flogged the ticket on to some other unsuspecting snake, who was happy to take it off my hands for a ton, as I'd told him I'd been barred from the bookies over another incident, he lapped it up and I disappeared into the night.

Little did I know but that opportune incident would play a key part in my eventual downfall. Somebody had seen me, someone who knew me. I never found out who and I can see why they wouldn't stand for that kind of crime, the kid didn't deserve to lose his money or get cracked like that. Who knows his story, recently laid off from the pit, perhaps; maybe a stroke of luck meant he could clear his debts and take the kids on holiday, you never know, but I was young and I did what I did anyway.

That was the start of my downfall, that and some of my other recent crimes. The Police knew I was up to no good, they were just biding their time, making sure when they did me 'proper' so that I was going away for a while.

LYCEUM JEWELLERS

'The Blag'

You could say this was the first 'serious' blag I was involved in, the first one I'd been pulled for in any event. By serious you know what I mean, the type that makes The Sheffield Star, the type that is the talk of the high street, spreading like wildfire around the city and on to the outlying estates.

I was only about nineteen at the time, I'd pulled together a little team and planned a smash and grab on the Lyceum jewellers in Sheffield City Centre. The posher area of town, renowned for plays, theatre, fine dining and all that middle-class stuff that us Manor lads never appreciated. The Theatre is still there and steeped in history, but the jeweller's is long gone, but that wasn't my doing.

It was to be a brazen 'smash and grab', the type you'd see in the old gangster movies or even newspaper cartoon strip, all I was missing was the striped jumper and swag embossed bag over my shoulder.

The team on this one consisted of me, my good childhood friend Nicky Froggatt and a couple of older guys Tony Canetti and another kid who acted as the driver, Mick Barker. They weren't close acquaintances, but lads who had access to a half decent motor, which was rare back then. Even rarer was the fact that they were willing to be involved in an outrageous stunt like this.

This particular heist didn't involve my mentor Dave Lee. I was working with a couple of firms at the time, and wasn't choosy, there was no need to involve Dave on this one, in fact as it would turn out I was doing him a favour by not involving him. This job was my brain child, one I'd later regret. I was the key man on this one, I'm not even sure why the others got their cut, but I needed their assistance to avoid any problems during my escape.

A week before we'd planned out the job to make good my escape. The ideal place to have the car was about a quarter of a mile away, the distance was no issue to me but one section in particular was a cause for concern. There was a short stretch through a subway on my escape route, and I needed to ensure I wasn't headed off at the pass. I'd assessed the route and that was the only point at which I would be vulnerable. So Mick Barker our driver was waiting about a quarter of a mile away in the trusty old Blue Volvo and the other two, Froggatt and Canetti, manned both ends of the Subway so that no one could take me down either side of the daylight.

The day had arrived. It was half past three on a Saturday afternoon, the high street was still packed, and I mean it was chock-a-block with people. We were ready to make our move. There was no CCTV back then I didn't feel the need to mask up, that would only arouse more suspicion and eat into my precious escape time, if someone called the Rozzers before I'd even made it to the shop window. The world was a much smaller place back then and the chances of me being eye-balled by someone who knew me in that part of town were slim, as daft as that may sound. You only ventured into town maybe a couple of times a year from our neck of the woods; those on the estate could unlikely afford a visit to the high end Lyceum area of town, they had no reason. The only way you were gonna get nicked was if somebody who categorically knew you, saw you, and furthermore if they were willing to point the finger. With our reputation this was always deemed low risk. How wrong we were on this particular occasion. I guess in some respects we thought we were invincible. I was soon to find out that I wasn't.

Like I'd mentioned before, my natural athleticism always came to the fore. I really was that fast and by my own assessment, the member of the gang most suited to pulling this one out of the bag. Once I had that loot in my hands no one was catching me outside of the Olympic squad. If only their scouts had been around to see me run that day I'd have been destined for selection for the four hundred metres.

"Right lads, you know the plan." And with that we all headed off to our pre-agreed individual locations to form part of our overall plan.

I waltzed up to the window no different to any of the other weekend shoppers, except at my side was a house brick concealed in an old, inconspicuous, Co-op carrier bag (that'd be 5p on expenses these days).

I took one last glance in either direction, just on the off chance that any old bill were passing by and took a gulp of courage.

CRAAAAAAASH! I launched it straight through the shop window. It went through with an ease that surprised even myself and not really saying much for the expensive security glass that the insurance companies demanded on those kind of places. It shattered into what seemed like a million pieces, equal amounts strewn inside the shop display cabinet and the street outside.

At the very moment the glass crashed through into the shop, I saw a face of sheer shock looking right back at me - a bloke (the Sales Manager) a couple of feet from my face with only fresh air separating us now. I could smell his breath he was that close. He was left looking out dumbfounded from the other side. I'd frightened him to death, like a rabbit in the headlights. He knew what was happening, but his faculties were subdued from the shock, not allowing him to react, it didn't matter even if he had been able to.

I quickly grabbed the two prominently positioned Omega 'Golden Eagle' watches and a tray of gold ingots, precisely the items I'd come for, nothing more nothing less. This had to be a flash theft, there was no time for greed or deliberation on what to take. I'd eye balled what I wanted the day previous and that's precisely what I took. Gold values were relatively high at the time, we knew what the score was going to yield, or thereabouts, maybe the watches would be a little harder to get the right money for, but gold is gold, and usually had a fixed rate per kilo attached to it even in the criminal world. One that we wouldn't struggle to obtain with our contacts in the fencing game.

I was off like a bullet, in my mind out to smash that Borstal Race Course record all over again, jumps the lot, nothing would stop me from getting away. That place had served me well. I ran the hundred or so yards down the street and took a swift left around the corner, another couple of hundred yards and I hit the subway, its entrance being guarded by my good pal Nicky Froggatt. He legged it down the tunnel with me, towards Canetti who was manning the other end. It was a ghost tunnel, not a soul down there, just the trampling stampede of our footsteps resonating throughout the hollow core of the tunnel.

We emerged back into daylight and legged it the remaining stretch down the road and around the corner where the car was waiting. That old blue Volvo was ideal for the job, not by modern day standards, but my man Barker knew how to make it fly. There was far less congestion on the roads in those days, and only those with a few quid had motors, and that's exactly what we'd just earned ourselves, even the police didn't have an abundance of motors to chase us down if needed.

I know I've made this sound a little amateur, but there was always an element of planning, it wasn't so spur of the moment as I've made it sound. I'd been past and checked the window the week previous, even given it a little tap, the resonance giving me some indication of whether this was a goer, the high-pitched ping confirming my preferred outcome... it was going through without problem with any heavy object of my choosing, a cosh, bat, brick, it didn't really matter. We'd also decided exactly what we wanted (the two Golden Eagle watches, which were worth a few grand each along with a tray of Ingots). I fancied one of those watches myself, but the cash would be more handy; maybe one day I'd own one, who knew.

We'd already found a local buyer who could fence the gold and the watches. Gold was never a problem, the watches might be a little trickier with their inherent serial numbers - if anything caught us out it would be them.

We carved up the spoils, a few grand, which wasn't bad for a few hours work, while the rest of the world was being laid off. I'd taken the brunt of the risk, showing my face on the high street, but I still wasn't too concerned and we took our equal share of the spoils and went our separate ways.

I was later to find out the sale of those items was to be our undoing, something we'd later regret, or at least wish we'd taken more care with. Maybe taken things a little further afield, lord knows we had the contacts.

We'd sold the lot to a local fence, who eventually bubbled us to save his own skin on some other charges. It turned out the guy who'd paid us for the Lyceum goods was under some pressure from the local police for some 'other charges'. He was being pressed and needed a fall guy (or four) to improve his position. That would be us. He didn't know us that well, though I can't condone grassing, I guess it doesn't mean a lot if you're looking out for number one, and dropping someone you don't really know in the shit, and that's what happened.

THE CARTOON JUDGE

'Mr. Pickles RIP'

Up to this point, things had been ticking over nicely. It was early 1980, I was only nineteen years old, sleeping sound and living well with a few quid in my pocket. I even had my own motor parked on the drive of number ten Noehill Road, not everyone on the estate could say that back then.

Life was pretty sweet to say the least. I'd steadily become, in my eyes, somewhat invincible, pulling off the kind of heists that 'real' criminals did; blagging jewellers, jumping in getaways cars, the whole nine yards. A far cry from nicking a few loaves of bread down the local Co-op back in the late sixties and pocketing the few shillings I'd been given by my mother for the errand.

I was untouchable, or so I thought. But even in the world of criminality there are apprenticeships to be served, and that usually includes, as a minimum, a brief stint in prison. Although I thought I'd elevated to the major league I was soon to find out the hard way that you only ever learn from your own mistakes. My level of activity and blasé attitude towards the law could not be maintained for much longer. In this game you can only ever truly trust yourself, but that wasn't always conducive with getting shit done so we usually worked as a team. But with criminals someone always eventually opens their mouth that little bit too wide, especially when their back is against the wall, and that's exactly what brought about my (our) downfall.

After 'the wheels had fallen off', the interviews concluded and I was left to contemplate the outcome of the investigation. As in most cases it was referred to the CPS and, as expected, I was remanded pending trial. I'd expected no less, the evidence was more than damning and Wilson wouldn't have rested until I was locked up, even on lesser charges. He (Wilson – CID) informed me I would be shipped off to a place called Thorp Arch, over near Tadcaster, not somewhere I'd even heard of, to spend time on remand until my trial came up. I was thrown in the back of the meat-wagon, no camera flashes through the darkened windows like I'd seen on the local news, just empty silence.

Moments later we were making our way up the A1 north towards Tadcaster, rattling from pillar to post in the back of that mobile prison unit, the situation was starting to sink in.

Thorp Arch was a remand centre reserved exclusively for young prisoners (YPs). Whilst there my time on remand passed slowly, slower than it had ever done anywhere before. The court case looming over me, I felt like I was waiting to be hung, 20 years previous that might just have been the case. They used Thorpe Arch as an allocation centre, from there they'd decide which young offender's nick you would ultimately be sent to. Here I was, not even convicted and I was being held in an allocation centre, that said it all to me.

Though we were all YP's and of a similar age in Thorp Arch, I'd elevated above my peers and the other lads in my own age range. Most were in for petty misdemeanours or drunken mistakes. My impending record spoke for itself. I wasn't in for the usual misdemeanours of a lad my age. I was associating with hardened criminals and operating in a planned criminal manner. Not Saturday night spur of the moment drunken antics, it was premeditated and that made me different to the lads around me and meant I was destined for real gaol in the next year or so.

The screws had also realised this. They say the devil makes work for idle hands and as time passed I found myself getting into a few small but pointless problems, playground scuffles if you like, petty thefts, ones which would have been avoided if I'd had some focus, but nothing serious enough to influence the sentencing at my upcoming trial.

* * * *

The day of reckoning had arrived - the wheels were about to well and truly fall off. After a couple of months on remand, my hearing date was upon me. A thousand thoughts raced around my mind as I was shipped across Yorkshire and back to the Sheffield courts to face trial along with my counterparts Froggatt, Canetti and Barker, the team from the Lyceum job, and Dave Lee from the Haulage firm owner's burglary. It was a relief to see them all again as I entered the holding area.

We were all about to stand trial together for a plethora of crimes, but none was about to take the hit that I was. I was the only one implicated in all three crimes and an extra one of my own to boot. It had all been wrapped up into one trial. This wasn't the norm but the CPS had taken it down that route to save on court costs, a shrewd move and one that would win the hearts and minds of the tax-paying, some law abiding, citizens of Sheffield, the same ones sporting their cheaply purchased Omega watches and diamond rings and drinking in the celebratory rounds down the Springwood.

The trial had been something of a white wash, we were presented with evidence to which we had no reply, fingerprints, positive sightings, credible witnesses, the lot; every one of us was facing the shovel of some varying length.

My situation was the most extreme, I'd involved myself in all three incidents, the only way anyone else was coming off worse than me was via their pre-existing reputation, and that could only be the infamous Dave Lee. Judge Pickles had undoubtedly sentenced him before and he would undoubtedly want to hit him even harder this time. Though he must secretly have known that no sentence would ever deter a man of such criminal leanings a man who had once attempted to burn off his own fingerprints for the good of his criminal career.

I found myself standing in front of the infamous Judge Pickles. He was a notorious bastard, for want of a better term. In the eyes of the criminal fraternity, he was the Tom to our Jerry. He would deal with me and any other no good criminal swiftly and harshly, I had no doubt about that. This man took justice personally, I may as well have burgled his own house or mugged him on the way back from his chambers, NO ONE was getting off lightly when he was in charge. That's how it should be; good old fashioned crime and punishment, only a small step down from corporal, a true deterrent. Not that I thought that way at the time, but I know from being a career criminal myself that nothing more than brutal sentencing will stop most habitual criminals.

Judge James Pickles, was in a grand tradition of outspoken and colourful British judges, both real and fictional, prepared to expose the law to ridicule to try and reform it. His antics in the courtroom led some to suspect he might even be make-believe. Lord Chancellor Hailsham, described him as "a figure of fun, too ridiculous to exist". Pickles presented himself as the people's judge, the Yorkshire man versus London, the radical versus the fossils, but he still never took any leniency on us Yorkshire folk; he was a man of principle.

When they'd told us we were up in front of Pickles, all four of our hearts sank. That coupled with the damning evidence that was about to be served up against us made me pray the ground might swallow me up.

It turned out that when one of the guys had taken the Golden Eagle watches to be sold the guy who'd bought them, a well known and respected fence had found himself on bail for other offences himself and was looking to take the heat out of his situation and earn a few brownie points. He'd dished out names like Smarties. He owed us no favours, he wasn't a close friend or a regular associate. But in our line of business you just didn't do that, it was about reputation and repeat business, you can only shit on someone once. How can your friends trust you when you do something like that? We'd also been seen on the Lyceum job by a guy who knew us, and for some reason was willing to attest to that, deals sprang to mind, it wasn't the 'done thing' back then.

They also had my fingerprints for the burglary and an eye witness on the mugging on the way back from the bookies. I was bang to rights, a guilty plea was the only thing that could soften the blow.

My Barrister, David Adams, tried to get me a return to Borstal, he had to try something, as I was only nineteen years of age it was an option, but Pickles would never have that. He knew it and I knew it, these were mister's crimes and I belonged in a mister's gaol. Pickles peered over his glasses and shook his head in dismay.

"Not this time Broughton! You will get a 'real' custodial sentence this time." He proclaimed.

"Mr Broughton you are no longer a youth. You are willing to involve yourself in the activities of men and therefore you shall suffer the consequences like a man." He continued.

My legs began to buckle, I'd known this was coming, but now it was really getting the better of me.

"I sentence you to 4 years for both the robbery and the burglary." He started.

The next word I wanted to here was 'concurrent.' Please be 'concurrent', not the other word 'con'.... I couldn't even think it, never mind say it.

"And 3 years to run consecutively for the robbery on the young man from the bookmakers. A 6 months extension shall apply, as a result of your previous misdemeanours, making it seven and a half years in total." His face lighting up as he applied the icing to the custodial cake.

I can do basic maths your honour, I thought. I would have appreciated a cut to the chase in this particular instance, not a lesson in mathematics.

Pickles had felt the need to be extra harsh, when it had somehow come out that we'd robbed the haulage yard owner's place after seeing the date and time of a family member's funeral in the local paper, which was stooping low even by my standards.

I genuinely didn't expect what I got; I thought maybe a four, but not seven and half! But that was that.

Judge Pickles has since passed away. He died on 18 December 2010 and the harsh principles of real justice died with him. Despite our run-ins, I can solemnly say the British justice system is a much blander arena without him and in truth I am forever in his debt. I'm sure he's up there somewhere looking down on me wishing he could send me down one last time.

In the end, I'd got the biggest sentence of us all for playing the biggest part, I'd been more prominently involved in the bigger raids and the bookies stunt was my own, the other lads got three years each. I couldn't complain. I'd known what I was letting myself in for.

My day had come, from that day forward I wouldn't see daylight again for the next four years and ten months.

Rest in Peace Judge John Pickles.

GAOL

'Swinfen Hall via Armley'

Judge Pickles had laid down the law and made it clear I would not see any chance of parole for at least the first three years of my sentence, which was no worse than I expected, but I was also under no illusion and that any parole review would probably prove fruitless, if he had a hand in it.

I was destined for Swinfen Hall, Staffordshire, a Young Prisoner (YP) centre for those with the pleasure of being sentenced to longer terms. For a YP my term was up there with the best of them. I'd dived straight in at the deep end. Most lads my age who were getting sent down had just made a silly mistake or been caught up in a couple of small misdemeanours, not me, apart from the more sinister types of crimes I'd covered the whole spectrum, but in the main robbery and violence.

Unfortunately for me there was a waiting list to get in to Swinfen Hall so my first port of call was the notorious Armley Prison in Leeds. It was only intended to be a stepping stone to my true destination at Swinfen Hall, but became my first taste of a real mister's gaol, in the form of a short stay on its notorious 'D' Wing, again reserved for Young Prisoner's.

'HM Prison Leeds is a Category B men's prison, located on Gloucester Terrace in Leeds (LS12) in West Yorkshire. It opened in 1847 and to most is simply known as 'Armley'. Well known throughout the country as one of the toughest prisons in the UK. Still very archaic in its appearance and workings, it remains a Victorian stronghold, the rules and regimented routine still ingrained in its decrepit walls. It certainly wasn't any holiday camp, unlike some of the others I ended up at.

It was especially hard as a YP, we'd often be dragged in for a kicking or 'some fist' off the screws, we were easy targets. That behaviour just didn't wash with the older, more established prisoners, but us young lads were fair game. Maybe it was the deterrent needed to stop kids like us from re-offending, maybe Swinfen Hall wasn't really full at all and we were just sent there to get a taste of what real prison life would be like if we didn't mend our ways. The sad fact is, they'd have to be a lot harsher than that to deter me.

The younger prisoner's on 'D' Wing were kept well away from the real long term crooks in Armley, to avoid bullying, intimidation, coercion, but most of all networking. If a YP could be shown the error of his ways and returned to society knowing little more of criminal ways than when they arrived then all the better, but if he mingles, he learns, he gains associates and starts friendships that are often continued on the out. Plans are hatched and criminals blossom, and I am living proof of that.

I fitted straight in there, just like I had at Borstal, making our own entertainment to help the days pass. We'd hear of all these notorious criminals and prisoners, ones we were made aware to steer clear of.

I'd really landed on my feet at Armley, as it happened my pals Dave Lee, Steve Bagley and Sykesy were also in there on the main wings and had got Barry Walker in reception wrapped around their little finger. They'd instructed him to look after me and I became a very privileged YP indeed.

Good old Barry Walker used to fetch half a bucket of milk and a 'gret' block of cheese down to my cell every 'neet' and I'd even been allowed down the gym to train with the older cons, which was usually out of the question, as they looked to keep the YP's away from the older influence. The other YPs must have thought I was some kind of descendent from royalty, while they were wasting away I was growing every day. I never got any trouble in Armley, once people knew who my associates were I was untouchable.

Even the days when I was stuck on 'D' Wing I'd manage to give a fleeting shout out to my pals on the real wings, Dave Lee and his good pal and mine the boxer Paul Sykes. They'd always give me a shout back and as stupid as it sounds I felt a longing for the harsher environment they were in.

While I was in Leeds, the Black Panther was in, the guy who killed Lesley Whittle. Real name Donald Neilson aka the "Black Panther", he was an armed robber, kidnapper and murderer. He'd murdered three people during robberies of sub-post offices between 1971 and 1974, and also murdered his kidnap victim Lesley Whittle, an heiress from Highley, Shropshire. He had been sentenced to life imprisonment in July 1976. There were rumours flying around that the IRA wanted him out, for whatever reason, so he was under heavy guard nearly all of the time. Good luck with that one, Leeds nick was a genuine fortress; I couldn't see anyone managing to get out.

One day me and some of the other young lads waiting to be moved on were pissing around in our cell. We'd opened the hatch to watch some of the characters passing through, hoping to see someone we knew or some minor celebrity of the criminal world when I caught a glimpse of the guy, The Black Panther, I knew who he was from the press coverage and the manhunt that had been undertaken to bring him to justice.

I shouted "Donald! Donald" Like we were on first name terms already, well I doubt he answered to his moniker of 'The Black Panther', that might be deemed an admission of guilt.

He ran over a couple of steps to see who it was, assuming it had to be someone he knew 'on the out', my friendly Yorkshire tone luring him in.

He went "What?" In his, now fading, Yorkshire accent.

I went "Have you seen Leslie Whittle hanging about anywhere?" Hitting him where it hurt.

His face turned a bitter shade of crimson in embarrassment and we all burst out laughing. The so called Panther wasn't impressed with my Borstal Boy prank, but what could he do, shackled up and a prison door preventing his path. The screws hated him anyway, and joined in the chorus of laughter at my childish prank.

Regardless, I'd have my fingers crossed I wouldn't encounter the Black Panther again further down my sentence.

That spell at Armley passed quickly and it wasn't long before I was moved on to my intended destination, Swinfen Hall. I didn't get the opportunity to fully appreciate it that time around but Armley, Leeds has to be the worst prison in the north and probably in the UK, but I knew I'd be back to see it's true colours before long.

* * * *

After that relatively short spell at Armley of about five months I arrived at Swinfen Hall, near Lichfield in Staffordshire. HM Prison Swinfen Hall is, or was, a Category 'C' men's prison and Young Offenders Institution, located in the village of Swinfen and named after Swinfen Hall which stands opposite the main prison. It opened in February 1963 as a Borstal and in 1972 became a long-term young offenders' institution.

After my little stop off at Leeds I found myself in what could only be described as a bit of a holiday camp, much like Borstal, full of snotty nosed pretenders and not where I really wanted to be. I'd made my decision to knuckle down, give myself the best possible chance of parole and prayed I'd be out much sooner than my full term. I quickly made the screws aware of my sporting capabilities and within no time at all I was made gym orderly, a position I relished.

One day a screw approached me and gave me a word of advice. It might surprise you, but I was a good con in many respects, never a nuisance to the screws, I just got on with my time, my chores and generally followed orders. The Prison Officer approached me and told me they were doing a course on Anatomy and Physiology very soon, which tied in nicely with my love of sports.

"Why don't you take it? You'll get parole much sooner that way, it shows willing, trust me," He said.

With hindsight I should have taken his promises with a pinch of salt. Pickles would still have influence in any of my outcomes and he would never allow a scally like me to get off lightly, reformed or not.

The course was twelve months and I'd already done about eighteen by this time. I thought for a Prison Officer to say that to me, he knew something from the inside, maybe the Governor had tipped him off.

I saw the course through, came out with an 'O' Level, Grade One and within a month I was up for my parole hearing. My fingers were tightly crossed, but given I'd been following the advice of a trusted screw I had some confidence that things might go my way.

Not a fucking chance! I went up for parole and got a straight knock-back. I was gutted. I felt truly let down, I'd also got my, then, bird's hopes up, in fact she'd waited about three years for me to get out, she ended up fucking off with a kid who I know, a European Champion at Karate, I wasn't going to pursue that one when I got out. My mum and dad and the rest of the family had all got their hopes up as well, I was beyond deflated.

By this time I'd reached twenty-one, that little administrative kick in the bollocks had tipped me over the edge and I was ready to be starred up. I was that pissed off with the outcome of my hearing I walked straight into the Governor's office and made my wishes known.

I said, "Listen I want to go to the fuckin man's gaol now, I've had enough of this playground. I want making up." His eyes nearly popped out his fucking head, a YP asking to be thrown to the sharks.

"I don't belong here with all these kids. I want to be made up to mister's gaol. I don't fit in around here and I'm of an age now". He couldn't believe what he was hearing.

"I understand," The Governor said, "Let me see what I can do."

He knew I was ready as much as I did. He understood my predicament and knew I deserved to get something of what I wanted for my efforts, so he helped sanction the move and my transfer to the real prison world.

In all honesty I just wanted to be in a place with some of my friends from the outside world, Dave Lee, Sykesy, Steve Bagley and a couple more who I knew were still in Armley, that would have been the ideal. I knew it was a gamble, there was no assurance I was heading for Armley and as a young, impressionable lad if the Governor got wind I wanted to be around those types of people there wasn't a cat in hell's chance I'd be in the same county as them, never mind the same prison.

Within a week I was on the bus and on my way to Walton, Liverpool. I knew there were a few 'friends of friends' in there and I'd get a good welcome. My wish had been granted and I was hurtling down the M6 to my new home in Liverpool.

SOCCER IN THE LOCK-UP

'Walton Prison – Starred Up'

After my knock back for parole aged just twenty one, for reasons which they never chose to divulge, my demands to be transferred to a 'real' prison were met. They'd sent me on to Walton Prison in Liverpool, a long term re-allocation centre. Though I pleaded to be sent back to Leeds they were having none of it.

HM Prison Liverpool (formerly known as Walton Gaol) is a category B/C local men's prison in Walton, Liverpool. It opened in 1855 and houses around eleven hundred prisoners.

Most people wouldn't dream of asking to be upgraded, for want of a better term, from a YP nick to a real mister's gaol, but I'd had enough. It might sound strange but I was glad to find myself in the surroundings of a real prison with people I could relate to. I had hoped to be sent back to Armley, where I knew my pals Dave Lee, Steve Bagley, Sykesy and their associates were currently residing, but Walton would do for now. As a bonus though it probably had the best football pitch of all the prisons in the country, or so I'd been told, and that helped soften the blow.

When I first arrived the faces wandering the landing were unfamiliar to me, but I made an effort to converse and managed to break the ice with a few of the more 'well known' villains residing there. I wasn't one for name dropping generally, but if it made my stay more comfortable and day to day life easier then it was a no brainer. I made sure to let people know I was a good pal of Dave Lee and Sykesy and I was immediately accepted into the right circles. Some of the 'names' were happy to associate with me and took me under their wing, which would hopefully lead to extended gym privileges as well, just like at Armley.

It was at Walton I first met the likes of Delroy Showers and Jimmy Tagoe from Liverpool, Davy Glover and the Tamm's (Arthur and Tommy) from Newcastle, John Wynn from Manchester and Billy Barnes from Leeds, to name but a few. All known faces, but all new to me. Though Delroy I'd met briefly as a kid in the Springwood in Sheffield, when he'd turned up accompanied by the notorious Paul Sykes. I quickly began to realise that these people, who were from every corner of the country I might add, had only ever met in the nick prior to the day they converged on the Springwood. You could see how the country becomes a much smaller place once you're inside, suddenly you have friends from all over, and each one knew a trick that the other didn't and you could see why the authorities wanted to stamp out those associations.

Delroy Showers was always one of my favourite characters and a great friend. He was a real criminal Kingpin from the Liverpool underworld, an international man. Not your average mouthy scouser, an educated man with a penchant for the other more feminine inmates, one he wouldn't even deny himself, but you better believe he was to be taken seriously. At the time he was doing nine years for drug importation, his brother Michael was also well known within the system. Upon my arrival I made a conscious effort to go speak to him and let him know that I was from Sheffield and a close pal of Dave Lee and Sykesy. That instantly made my stay a little easier.

Sykesy was somewhat of a legend of Walton nick for one very bizarre reason. Still a YP at the time, aged just nineteen, he'd skinned the prison cat. The story has it that the screws used to feed the cat a man's rations every day and this didn't sit well with Paul. He'd promised the other lads that he would get rid of it, his logic being if he got rid of the cat then there'd be more food to go round for everybody. When he'd been hauled in by the prison governor at the time for the murder of the prison cat, he reeled off the twenty one prison rules and made it clear there was nothing in there about not skinning cats. Reluctantly the Governor had to agree, but it marked his card for some time to come.

Anyway, Delroy took to me immediately, affectionately nicknaming me 'Nephew', a comical reference to the fact that he was as black as the ace of spades and I was a fair haired, pale skinned youngster without a hint of anything other than Sheffield in my blood. We became great friends throughout that stay. I knew his brother Michael as well, though not nearly as well. I'd heard rumours he'd chopped somebody's head off, and more to the point he'd gotten away with it, I had my doubts how true that was, but you never know, but it got mentioned from time to time in the prison yard.

To hear Del speak in his eloquent scouse / West Indian take on the Queen's English you would struggle to guess why he was even in prison, in fact you'd assume it was an absolute injustice on face value. But looks can be deceiving and he was a certified criminal, one of the highest up the chain, I was under no illusion, he liked me, but I would never make it into his working circle, there are levels in all games.

Del had been one of my best pals on that sentence. Although a fair bit older than me, he introduced me to Power-Lifting in the prison gym. His seemingly effortless physique was to be admired, while I broke my back in the early stages learning to power lift he carried the weight of an Ox like it was nothing. He was short, and looked nothing at first glance, but underneath he was solid, with masses of thick muscle. He didn't smoke or drink and trained almost every day.

The great thing about Walton was there were more opportunities to play football than in most other nicks. I'd assume my usual position up front and teach the rest of the nick how it was done. There was the odd semi-talented player in their but most were out just to kill the time of day, not me. I loved football it meant more to me than the average con.

I'd be flying down the wing, trying to get on the end of crosses like my life depended on it, in my head I could hear the taunts and cheers coming from the touchline just like a Sunday morning down the Manor, but it was all in my head. I'd turn around and see a fat old slob of a screw or hear the bark of the prison guard dog and reality would kick back in.

Every now and then I'd hear Del from the sidelines.

"Come on Nephew, put it away" He'd scream. While the other cons looked around in bemusement wondering what the fuck he was going on about. How could this skinny little white kid possibly be his nephew?

Those precious moments, a half hour here and there, made the concrete walls of the prison disappear, and if they had I wouldn't have run for the hills, my competitive desire would have kept me within those chalked lines whether I liked it or not.

I ended up spending a total of eight months at Walton before being moved on to my dispersal jail, one which would surprise most.

Though he wasn't one for football himself Delroy would often come and watch the makeshift prison matches and unknowingly to he once penned a poem about my skills on the pitch, a wondrous play on words that would have you think it were a FA Cup semi-final, it simply read…

Soccer in the Lock-up
(Liverpool Prison circa-1983)

Refurbed and gleaming prison-walls.......

Razors welded to giant snaked-wires.......

German-shepherd wolves herd us all.......

We thirst our freedoms in Match Day High......

No beer here in Walton-jail's Kop......

Yet azure-blue skies give game-day glow.......

And come we all to stand-in-awe.....

Of Mighty Clyde Broughton in full-flow.......

Striker, Midfield or solid Back.......

He's Carl Lewis so runs like Easy.......

210-pounds of power-lifters fury.......

Brother Clyde Broughton YORKIST GLORY!

Delroy Whitfield-Showers

FRAGGLE ROCK

'Dispersal'

HMP Wakefield is a Category 'A' men's prison, located in Wakefield, West Yorkshire and is the largest high-security prison in the UK and indeed Western Europe. Nicknamed "Monster Mansion" due to the large number of high-profile, high-risk sex offenders and murderers held there, we preferred to call it 'Fraggle Rock.'

As my sentence gradually neared its end I was sent to Wakefield Prison. I say sent, I actually asked to go to Wakefield as it was the nearest / most convenient dispersal location to me and much easier for my visitors to get to. I should imagine not many people have ever asked to be moved there, and even if they had, not many would be granted that wish, but I did and I was.

Wakefield houses up to five hundred lifers, can you imagine such a place? While I was in Wakefield I encountered every walk of the criminal life - robbers, burglars, fraudsters, rapists, nonces, you name it. You hear how Bronson is the worst prisoner in the country, well he may have caused the screws a few problems over the years, but his crimes were nothing of the level of some of the scumbags I lived alongside in that place. They always used to say, "When there's nothing left to do with them in Broadmoor, send 'em to Wakefield." There were some real monsters in there and some real characters, and winding them up certainly helped pass the time of day for the more sane amongst us.

One con that springs to mind was called De Havilland, a sinister sex case who was in the cell next door to me. It's amazing you look these people up now and they're very hard to find any information on, but there were some real nasty creatures in there. We used to wind him up a treat. You'd often hear rumours of what people had done, but one day I found out the truth about him.

I shouted over to him in the next cell, "Oi lad, lend us ye fanny mags." With a snigger.

He replied, "I haven't got any" As though he was the most clean living wholesome con on the landing.

I said, "Well give us your depositions instead, I'll have a wank over them," A twisted joke over what he'd heard he was in for. A deposition is a witness's sworn out-of-court testimony. It is used to gather information as part of the discovery process and, in limited circumstances, may be used at trial.

Well bugger me, if he didn't pass them over. It wasn't so funny when I read them and realised the things we'd heard about him were all true. He had followed a woman off the bus, got through her kitchen window and raped her on top of her husband with a knife to her throat and then done him as well. Crazy Shit! One of the most horrific crimes I've ever heard of and this freak barely made the papers. Not much comes up about him on the net, but bizarrely I was later to encounter him again, further down the line, under another guise and in another gaol.

Monster Mansion was a strange place come night time, once all the fruit loops have had their medication from the dispensary. They'd all be stood outside their cells expressionless. You'd say "Alreyt" and get no response, yet just a few hours earlier you'd been chatting to them clear as day. Now they'd be wandering around like Zombies! It was the easiest way for the system to retain control and most of these low lives were happy to go along with it, even they didn't feel like they were in prison when the meds kicked in.

The Governor at the time was a real bastard, and trust me it took a real bastard to run that horror house. Child murderer and sex offender Ian Huntley ended up there. Serial killer Dr. Harold Shipman also committed suicide at Wakefield Prison in 2004. If they're on the sick list then Wakefield is usually where they reside.

In some respects we used to police Wakefield prison ourselves, save the screws from getting the sack. We'd go round beating nonces up in that place just to pass the time of day. One of the guys, Mick Riley, who was part of our little nonce bashing gang, had gotten himself the perfect alibi by being on our squad; It turned out he was actually in for raping his babysitter. Obviously we didn't know and never questioned him too hard, as it never crossed our minds. You just didn't know who to trust in that place. He came unstuck one day when he was outed by one of the screws while we were barricaded up: "He's a sex case", "Fuck off! He's one of us." We all insisted. Turned out we were wrong.

I remember a young girl had been taken, raped and murdered in Dewsbury, an area close to the prison where a lot of the screws lived and their kids went to school. The guy who'd done it ended up in Wakefield, and obviously the screws weren't going to keep it hush, hush that close to home. In fact, it was a lot less than hush, hush - they actually used to give us cash for the privilege of knocking these beasts around.

Back then you were allowed to carry money, only coins, never paper. Payment would usually take the form of a stack of fifty pence pieces. It might sound like nothing, but it would often be around a tenner's worth of fifty pence pieces; this was 1982 and a tenner was a decent amount of money back then.

A lot of the time these little payments would come about if a nonce had been leery with one of the screws, the worst thing a nonce can do is wind up a screw, because indirectly they're going to get it back and no blood would be on the hands of the screw to point the finger or whinge to the governor.

Our weapon of choice back then was a bed or table leg from those prison tables that stood in the corner. The back leg used to come off without problem and it was as easy to swing as a bat. As soon as the screws opened the cell and walked off, they knew where we were headed.

Monster Mansion might sound bad, but I found Leeds worse in many ways. There you were banged up 23 hours a day, if it even looked like it was gonna rain you weren't allowed out. At Wakefield you had your association, you knew where you stood, you could pick your pals, which was a big deal amongst all those sex freaks. Don't let them pick you, you pick them, those were some wise words I received from a screw when I first arrived. Establish your setup early and make life comfortable.

When you first go in, day by day, you get to work people out, You might be talking to someone one day and they seem like a really nice kid and then in the next breath someone would come whisper in your ear, "Don't talk to that cunt he's a ...." You know how it goes. In prison, never take anyone on face value, like they say "What's a nonce look like?" I've seen them come in all shapes and sizes, the typical little weed with pervy glasses on right up to giant stocky fellas, the ones you assume are bouncers or rugby players.

A screw once pulled me to one side and said "Listen, don't be just doing them little 5' 4" ones, you need to take them all out, six footers, the lot of 'em."

Which we did, but it wasn't so easy with those big fuckers. Our saving grace being the tip off from the screw meant there wouldn't be any real repercussions for the punishment we dished out.

Wherever possible the screws turned a blind eye, they'd only nick you if they had to and it was usually when they'd not been informed it was gonna happen. We must have done at least fifteen to twenty on behalf of the screws while I was in there. I'm not saying the white shirts knew about it, the SO's and PO's, but the blue shirts definitely did. It was always in the back of your mind, were you being set up? When a screw you knew actually didn't like you asked you to do a nonce, it was a double edged sword, could I get nicked for it, thankfully it never happened.

One screw in particular was virtually 'one of the lads'. I remember one New Year's Eve, the Landing Screw Melvyn Moffat was in our cell sat on the end of the bed with us smoking weed and drinking hooch. I think there was about six of us in the cell. There wasn't a regular piss test or anything like that back then and they often used to let weed pass as they knew it would calm everyone down, or to some extent. You should have seen the state of him when he left our cell about fifteen minutes before bang up, he had a right wobble on, bleary eyed, his hat back to front the lot. We absolutely pissed ourselves laughing as he swayed down the corridor to clock off.

Wakefield was rammed with sinister characters. There were tales of one sex case in Wakefield who used to walk about with a young lasses fanny in his wallet. Honestly, you couldn't make this shit up, fucking disgusting. Another one was a Paki lad called Majid had caught his wife shagging another bloke, so he killed them both and started eating them. Then there was Red Riding Hood (Patrick). He used to have a wreath delivered to the jail every year, he was known to take kids into the woods and kill them, hence the nick name. Most people had never even heard of these people.

Alfie Fox was another, from the Pontefract area, he killed his ex wife, mother in-law and left a baby to fend for itself on the grass outside in the garden. They'd got him on circumstantial evidence, using hair fibres on a pillow, but he'd done it, trust me. I was padded up with him in

Wakefield, while I was on induction. I think his tariff was fifteen years, what the fuck was I doing in a cell with the likes of him? But I'd chosen that place for ease of visits for my family / friends and closeness to home for dispersal. He always pleaded his innocence, I was once out on association with him and once asked him "Who do you reckon is the most dangerous person amongst all these monsters in here?" And do you know what he said, "Me!" He looked like Peter Sutcliffe the cunt, dark hair, beard the lot. He spent a lot of time in the chokey put it that way. There was obviously some doubt about his guilt somewhere, maybe from the lack of 'real' evidence, but that doesn't mean he didn't do it. The police even came to see me when I'd got out, as they knew I'd shared a cell with him, to ask my opinion on whether I thought he was innocent or not.

You were put in a big three cell, like two cells knocked together. There was me, Alfie Fox and another guy called Andy Evans. He had killed his bird in the heat of the moment, not a calculated monster like most of the other guys on the wing, but a man who had been consumed by momentary madness.

One of my favourite characters from Wakefield and the epitome of a true gent was a guy by the name of Ramsay Shannon. He was convicted of the murder of Gisela Meyerat in Bournemouth on 27 July 1964. He'd first met her at the Studleigh Hotel where he worked. Gisela was a German girl from Hamburg and worked as a waitress. Ramsay had said their relationship was beautiful at first but when Gisela saw how jealous he was becoming she ended it. Ramsay vowed from that day forward that if she could not be his then nobody would have her and spent weeks secretly scheming how he would end her life.

Ramsay Shannon had a fairly extensive criminal record which included convictions such as housebreaking, larceny, obtaining credit by fraud, taking a motor vehicle, stealing a Power Rammer, GBH, stealing scrap metal, stealing growing fruit, possessing an offensive weapon and wounding with intent, to name just a few.

At the time he was on his second life sentence for stabbing his missus about sixty times, just to be sure. To meet him you would never believe it, he was so laid back about everything and boy did he give the screws, and sometimes the cons, the run-around. In truth he was a right weird bastard, but always the perfect gentleman.

One day we had to wait at the gates for our dinner. The Cat 'A' prisoners usually went first, accompanied by a screw, while we all waited starving. Ramsay was digging his heels in, he made the whole nick wait a good twenty minutes, 'fannying around' in his cell, always so laid back, he knew he was never getting out, he just didn't care.

So the screws eventually convinced him to hurry up and come down for his feed, ten minutes later he swaggered down like a soldier on parade. Everyone was really stressing out now. "Fuckin hell, Ramsay! Everyone's starving, waiting to get fed." A con shouted.

So Ramsay turned around to address the baying crowd and said, "Patience is a virtue, now wait another ten minutes, you will learn" And casually swanned off back up the stairs. Imagine the brass neck, the type of people he was pissing off and he didn't care one bit. Another of Monster Mansion's crazy characters. That's should give you an idea of what Wakefield and its residents were like back then.

54 DAYS SOLITARY

'Bobby 'Blue"

I generally kept my head down in that nick, kept in with the screws, did what made my life easiest, especially given I was so close to the finish line, but an incident occurred that could have been deemed a small set back.

So I'd found myself in Wakefield nick awaiting dispersal and while I was in there, there was another prisoner by the name of Robert Maudsley, possibly the most high security prisoner in British history. He's still in there now and probably will be forever. You must have heard of this cunt, Hannibal Lecter himself, Bronson wasn't a patch in terms of the levels of danger this guy presented.

Maudsley had killed one on the outside and to top it off continued on the inside, killing one in Broadmoor, and another two whilst in Wakefield itself, that's some serious shit if you stop and think about it.

For the safety of himself and others he was kept him in a cell within a cell. When you opened his cell door, there was a cage and they used to feed him through a hatch like a fucking dog. Every time he went anywhere in the jail, there had to be six screws escorting him at all times.

He was a queer, possibly not a real one, but a rent boy, luring punters in only to repay them with vengeance for the things his father had done to him in his early days. Something truly terrible must have happened to him as a kid for him to turn out like that, most likely getting shagged and beaten by his old man, not a good start in life.

One day, after a bit of an altercation with a screw, I'd gotten myself fifty four days down the block for barricading up. I'd come back from the gym and hadn't had time to shower, so I filled a wash bowl to the top, put it on the floor and proceeded to get myself sorted. I was in a three man cell at the time. One of the screws came up to the spy hole, but I was just out of sight getting washed.

He yelled in "Broughton, show your face!."

Well, I've got two eyes tattooed on my arse cheeks, so I turned round and showed him those instead. Needless to say he didn't see the funny side.

"You're fuckin nicked!" I wasn't walking the line but I wasn't exactly hurting anyone and the next thing I know me and my cellmates are barricaded up, unwilling to deal with the consequences of what was only a practical joke.

We were hauled up in there for a day and a half. The screws were begging us to open up. We'd pushed our cast iron beds up against the door and there was no way they were getting in. That same morning I was supposed to be on adjudication to the Governor, but you never went till late in the morning so I'd had time to get my breakfast, plenty of food and water. I was full enough to last a few more days if needed. The whole prison was shut down because of our actions, no visits etc. We agreed to come out if the board of visitors came to ensure our safety when we got out. By the time they came the whole nick was going crazy and when we eventually came out we had two screws and a dog to each one of us. We thought it was great, all the prisoners shouting at us, our fifteen minutes of fame.

For that little misdemeanour we each got 54 days solitary down the block. Thankfully, the cons let the incident blow over and there was no real retribution, just a few awkward stares.

So, now I found myself in solitary (confinement) and directly below me was a guy hauled up in a cell so tightly controlled / sealed, I thought it might contain the prison guard dog. There wasn't even room to get a hand in. What kind of fucking monster could possibly be in there. The external window barely had any ventilation at all.

I was on my way to the yard one day when I looked over and noticed there was something tucked away in the thin grove between the metals bars and the concrete sill. Whatever was in there had left us (me) a roll-up, a bit of baccy and some split matches. We weren't allowed to smoke down the block, whoever was in there was showing an act of kindness. I went over and grabbed them and shouted "Cheers".

"No worries" the call came back.

"What's your name?" I asked.

"Rob. You?" The voice came back.

"I'm Clyde. Cheers my friend." From then on whenever I was passing he'd shout me over "Clyde! Clyde" and we'd have little conversations about this and that and he'd sort me a smoke. I never really questioned who he was, he seemed mild mannered enough.

Then one day a screw had seen me walking away from one of those little conversations and he said "Do you know who that is you're talking to there?".

"No," I relied, "But he seems alrelyt"

"Alroyt!" He laughed. "That's fucking Robert Maudsley! He's a right dodgy bastard, don't talk to him" The Screw had said to me as he turned the key to the yard.

"He'll try talking to you. Just ignore him" He continued.

"If you shared a cell with him, you'd have to have fucking matches in your eyes when you go to sleep. He's killed more in this place than most of our prisoners have on the outside."

Fucking hell. I couldn't believe what I was hearing. It turned out Maudsley was a man of many nicknames. They'd first called him 'Blue' because that was the colour the face of his first victim had turned as he slowly strangled him. Then he became known as 'Spoons' after killing again and leaving the body with a spoon sticking out of the skull and part of the brain missing (allegedly). His third and fourth victims died on the same afternoon and soon afterwards Robert Maudsley acquired the nickname that has stuck: Hannibal the Cannibal.

Although he is now nearly fifty and has not committed a crime for more than twenty five years, Maudsley is officially classified as Britain's most dangerous prisoner, forget Bronson, this man is said to represent such a high risk to those around him that he has spent the past quarter of a century in virtual isolation. With no prospect of ever being released, he will remain in prison in that isolation until he dies.

Maudsley once wrote, "The prison authorities see me as a problem, and their solution has been to put me into solitary confinement and throw away the key, to bury me alive in a concrete coffin. It does not matter to them whether I am mad or bad. They do not know the answer and they do not care just so long as I am kept out of sight and out of mind. I am left to stagnate, vegetate and to regress; left to confront my solitary head-on with people who have eyes but don't see and who have ears but don't hear, who have mouths but don't speak. My life in solitary is one long period of unbroken depression."

Housed in a 'glass cage' directly below me, a two-cell unit at Wakefield prison that bears an uncanny resemblance to the one featured in The Silence of the Lambs. It was built especially for him in 1983, seven years before the film was released. At around 5.5m by 4.5m, the two cells are slightly larger than average and have large bulletproof windows through which he could be observed. The only furnishings were a table and chair, both made of compressed cardboard. The lavatory and sink were bolted to the floor while his bed was merely a concrete slab, they were leaving nothing to chance.

A solid steel door which opened into a small cage within his cell, encased in thick Perspex, with a small slot at the bottom through which the guards passed him his food and little else.

He remained in that cell for twenty three hours a day with only an hour of exercise per day, when he was escorted to the yard by six prison officers. He was not allowed contact with any other inmates. It was a level of intense isolation to which no other prisoner has ever been exposed. Apparently he has a genius-level IQ level, and from what I saw loved classical music, poetry and art.

During his last murder trial in 1979, the court heard that during his violent rages Maudsley believed his victims were his parents. The killings, his lawyers argued, were the result of pent-up aggression resulting from a childhood of near-constant abuse. Maudsley was born in June 1953, him and his siblings were all taken into care after they were found to be suffering from 'parental neglect'. The worst, however, was reserved for Robert. 'All I remember of my childhood is the beatings. Once I was locked in a room for six months and my father only opened the door to come in to beat me, four or six times a day. He used to hit me with sticks or rods and once he bust a .22 air rifle over my back.'

Declared unfit to stand trial, Maudsley was sent to Broadmoor hospital for the criminally insane and remained there for three years. What happened next has become the stuff of prison legend. In 1977 he and another psychopath took a third patient, a paedophile, hostage and barricaded themselves into a cell. They then tortured their victim for nine hours before garrotting him and holding his body aloft so that guards could see him through the spy hatch. According to one guard, the man was discovered with his head 'cracked open like a boiled egg' with a spoon hanging out of it and part of the brain missing.

Ironically, despite killing a patient in Broadmoor, Maudsley was found fit to stand trial. Convicted of manslaughter, he was sent not to hospital but to Wakefield Prison. He had been at the prison for only a matter of weeks when he set off on another killing spree. According to other inmates who were there at the time, Maudsley set out to kill seven people that day. The first was Salney Darwood, imprisoned for killing his wife. He lured him into his cell and cut his throat, then hid his body under his bed. Maudsley then spent the rest of the morning trying to find other people to lure back, but no one would go with him, "They could all see the madness in his eyes,". He then calmly walked into the wing office, placed a serrated homemade knife on the desk and informed the guards that they would be 'two short' when it came to the next roll-call, one of the friendlier screws Melvyn Moffat told me about that day

So, this guy was now my closest neighbour. Solitary meant being in my cell all day directly above his, no smoking but we were allowed the paper. Even the exercise yard was caged and we were only given a ball to boot about.

One day we we'd been having another one of our regular conversations. At that time there was a very real problem going on in the prison world with overcrowding, the demand for space was exceeding capacity, it seemed like they were locking people up for fuck all back then. How we got on to the subject I don't know but what Bobby came out with sent a shiver down my spine.

"You know how there could sort that problem, don't ye Broughts?" I was half expecting him to off reel off details of some reform policy or rehabilitation programme he'd been putting together during his hours of solitary.

"Fuck knows Bobby." I replied.

"Well I can think of a solution... Let me back up on the fucking landing. I'd sort that problem" Laughing, it was a joke, but one that sent a fucking shiver down my spine, as mild mannered as our conversation was I knew he fucking meant it. He'd have solved the overcrowding problem at Wakefield within a week, especially with all those nonces at his disposal.

A moment or two later the goose pimple subsided and I thanked the lord for the concrete that was separating us, thank god my time there was nearing an end.

FREE BIRD

'Released'

After the barricading up and stint in solitary I kept my nose clean, I was too close to the finish line to be getting my sentence extended. Time gradually passed and my release was imminent.

The big day had come. I threw on my tailor made suit and carried my standard issue green holdall bag, containing my life's possessions, and stepped out of the fortress gates.

Those sub-standard suits were issued to every prisoner upon release, made to measure from only the coarsest of materials, a fabric seemingly woven from camel pubes and barbed-wire. On paper they were given to prisoners to give them the best start back into the real world. Though in reality, and I was pretty sure, it was just to signal to anyone who didn't know who I was, that I was a con and not to be trusted, leaving thoughts to race around onlookers minds; what had he done that was so bad he had to wear that cheap suit? It must have been something pretty sinister, especially leaving the gates of Monster Mansion.

I wandered across town to the train station and made my way home to the bright lights of Sheffield with the small allowance I'd been given to get back on my feet.

I felt fantastic, over the moon in fact, a chance to start again, or more likely continue as I had, but with a little more intelligence and caution applied. I wasn't reformed by any stretch of the imagination, in fact I hadn't wanted to dent that small allowance I'd been given upon release and stole a couple of things from the newsagents on the train station platform, only a pre-packed sandwich and a chocolate bar but the signs were there I clearly hadn't found gaol the harshest of environments, not the wisest move, but I started as I meant to go on.

By the time I'd got out I'd served four years and ten months, I was twenty four years old and ready to re-establish myself, back in Sheffield on the Manor. Given I'd been sentenced to seven and a half years, I think we can safely say, in the main, I'd behaved myself in there. Why not? What's to be gained by not playing the game? Look at Bronson, I rest my case.

I'd been given six months parole, so they could keep an eye on me. I was bound over to stay at a halfway house, or hostel as it was, on Norfolk Park, Sheffield. My stay was intended to be used as a means to oversee my integration back into society, not that I needed it. But those were the terms of my release and if I didn't adhere to them I'd be back inside before I knew it.

That aside, I needed to get back 'bang at it' and bring some money in. I'd never struggled before and I didn't intend to now. Never happy with the constraints of a straight man's wage or indeed a fan of the hours, I knew it would only be a day or two before I reverted to the only thing I knew, villainy. The restrictions of the hostel didn't faze me nor did the consequences of resuming my criminal career. I'd accepted that prison was part of the villainy career path. The restrictions would simply mean I'd have to earn my crust during my hours of freedom under my curfew and make sure I could be found back at the hostel during the stated hours.

The Hostel wasn't all that bad, but I needed to get out. I'd briefly been seeing a local girl named Maggie. I basically used her to blag a council house. A mate of mine had set me up with her, but sadly we were really setting her up full stop. I needed a permanent address to get out of the hostel, so I made my probation officer aware I'd fallen head over heels in love and wanted to move in with her.

To make this happen the probation service would need to make a home visit to confirm my intentions. When they came out on the visit I'd placed all my football trophies out on the side, left my clothes lying around the house and bobbed four cans of lager in the fridge, all for effect. I knew it was cruel but Maggie was simply a means to an end, the leverage I needed to get out of the hostel. In any event I'd managed to convince my Probation Officer that things were genuine, and to some extent in Maggie's eyes they were and I was now allowed to leave the confines of the hostel and move in with her, on paper at least.

Soon after that I'd met Wendy, the real love of my life and it was done. This was the genuine thing. I'd spoken to her briefly after bumping into her at a nearby bus stop and then made positive moves to ask her out a week or so later, after bumping into her again down my old haunt the Springwood. I was besotted from the off and needed to find a way to bring us together. The problem was I was broke, absolutely skint, so I had to stoop just another notch lower and use Maggie's generosity to make it happen. I asked her if I could borrow a few quid to go see my mates over in Leeds. Unbeknownst to her I had actually arranged to meet Wendy for a drink, at where else? The Springwood, of course. That place has a lot to answer for.

We hit it off immediately, just like I knew we would, and the rest as they say is history. From that day forward it was me and Wendy all the way, whether I was on the out or banged up inside, she stood by me through thick and thin and for that she deserves a medal.

Luckily while I had been in Swinfen Hall my ex had put my name down for a house, which was normally a lengthy process, but the timing couldn't have been better. Within two months of getting out I had a house of my own and by

April 1985 me and Wendy were able to move in together and I was granted permission to ditch the hostel and my probation conditions altogether.

* * * *

Around this time my good pal Dave Lee was still locked up. He obviously didn't have the temperament to behave on that particular stint and me and Sykesy had begun to cement a more secure friendship on the outside.

Even though I hadn't encountered him much on that first stint, Paul's chats with Dave Lee made him fully aware that I was a decent lad and could be trusted. I made a point of going to visit him at the first opportunity. He was a good laugh to be around and hopefully he'd point me in the direction of a few quid.

I went through to see Paul on a few occasions in his beloved Wakefield. He travelled all over, but, when it came down to it, he was genuinely tied to that place, just like me and my beloved Sheffield. A few of those occasions stood out in my mind and mostly for their comedic value, Paul was a wind-up merchant to say the least, even though he had violence in his blood, to me, that wasn't his defining characteristic like some would have you believe, or it certainly wasn't during the times that I spent with him.

One time Paul's missus Cath had gone into labour and he'd rang me up and said "Come through, Clyde," I'll never forget I was sat watching Liverpool on telly at the time.

"Come through Clyde." He reiterated

I went "What for?" This is at 11 o'clock at night.

"Clyde," he said, "Our lass is in labour and I can't cope."

What was I going to do, turn up with hot towels and man the forceps? Anyway, I shot over to Wakefield and when I got there he went, "Do you want something to eat?"

"Yeah." I said, it seemed the haste and panic had subsided in him. So we ended up eating fucking goulash, seriously. It was all a bit surreal.

Then he asked, "Do you want a drink?"

"Of course." I replied.

"Come on then. Let's go into town." Bear in mind the reason he'd asked me to come over, lord knows how his mind worked.

So we got in my car and I thought, right, I'll park the car and we'll go to a club or something. We pulled up in town, "Wait here one minute." He told me.

So I'm sat in my car outside this club. He walked up to the doorman, said something and the Doorman's gone inside. Next minute he's come back with a crate of Red Stripe and handed it to Paul. Basically they were more than happy to give Paul whatever he wanted to keep him out of the place and that's how Paul got treated everywhere he went, to avoid the trouble that comes with the guy, they'd just give him what he needed to keep him happy and get rid. Even the screws used those tactics with him, and pretty much everywhere he went in Wakefield, be it the boozer, a club or the corner shop it was the same.

Another time I went through to see him with our lass and he went, "Come on Clyde. I've just gotta shoot over to Dewsbury to see somebody."

We set off to Dewsbury and ended up in bloody Blackpool, seriously! And everywhere you went with him and I mean everywhere, everything was for nothing. It wasn't all fear, I think some of it was respect. If these people ever needed a favour, Paul would be there to help out further down the line.

So, we were in Blackpool and he were fucking blind drunk by halfway through the day. As it turned out we were there to meet a guy by the name of Ronnie Threlfall. We walked into this pub and there happened to be a midget standing by the bar, only a few feet tall. Paul fucking ran up the midget, you should have seen the midget's face. He picked him up just like he was nothing, and went, "I'm entering the midget tossing competition. I want to practice with you!"

Fucking five minutes later, the midget's sat on his fucking knee. They're both having a right drink together, fucking brilliant! Camera phones weren't about then, but I wish they had been, some of the things I've seen him do were unbelievable.

On that occasion I'd left my missus Wendy with Paul's wife Cath. When we got back nearly twelve hours later they were both stewing. Wendy was positively growling, but deep down she knew what Paul was like and it was unlikely I'd instigated our little day out. I decided to make my excuses and headed back over to Sheffield to make the peace.

Paul also used to have a figure of his own head in his living room. Somebody had made the clay figure of Paul's head and given it to him, lord knows why, if you look closely it's the same one you can see in his house on the documentary 'Paul Sykes at Large.'

On one occasion I was over in Wakefield at Paul's place and he'd nipped out of the room, probably to the carzy, so I did a bit of Shadow Boxing on the clay model of his head for a laugh, he walked back in the room and caught me, "What the fuck are you doing Clyde?"

I had no real explanation to offer, then he saw the funny side and we both burst out laughing.

I'll always remember those trips over to Wakefield fondly and those little day trips he took me on. But it was time to knuckle down and start grafting again and Paul wasn't the one to do it with, he was too sporadic in his ways.

THE USUAL SUSPECT

'Identity Parade'

True I've done plenty of bird, but as an active villain it's par for the course and let me tell you there's plenty I've gotten away with over the years. But one incident involved a friend of mine and stands out a mile, because of the serious nature of the offence and the 'skin of the teeth' nature by which he'd gotten away with it.

It doesn't sit easy talking about these types of incidents, I am on the straight and narrow now, and so is my friend and, I would never wish to incriminate him, but this is what happened.

So I'll ask you, have you ever been stood in an identity parade? Probably not. Next question, have you ever been stood in an identity parade knowing you're guilty and the person about to identify you walks into the room, imagine it. Now imagine that person is so dim they can't even identify you. Well that's what happened to a friend of mine. God bless the man!

It started with a robbery, one where guns were involved, a very, very close encounter with the law that could have seen my friend with a serious sentence under his belt. There were three lads involved in that particular incident, I'd been invited but elected to sit that one out - I won't mention names this time as that's not my place, though I doubt at this point they'd mind too much, and hopefully they might get the chance to read this story, whether it be at home or in the prison library.

The word on the grapevine was that there was a significant amount of cash at a property out in the sticks. You'd be surprised what people squirrel away trying to save themselves a few quid from the prying eyes of the taxman, whether it be tradesmen, publicans, farmers, everyone was at it and who could blame them really.

It was a farmer's house. A middle aged guy who lived on his own, with rarely so much as a visit. Just him, his border collie, a few sheep and a load of fucking ducks. It turned out those ducks would have been more useful witnesses than the old farmer himself.

On this occasion the source of information was a reliable one and my friends were already looking forward to carving up the rewards, hopefully I'd see a pint out of it at some point when it was all over. Obviously in those types of instances the source of the information is as useful as any other member of the team on the job and just like the rest of them they'd be getting their cut when the job was done.

Like I said they'd been told there was a considerable amount of money on the premises. When I say considerable this was 1984 and rumour was there was thirty grand tucked away in that house, by today's standards that would be like landing a hundred grand.

My pals had headed up to the place, and as luck would have it the guy was stood outside in his field, only a little cunt, but you never knew with these little cunts, apparently he was a stocky bastard, as wide as he was tall, with a battered old red face that eluded his dependency for the whiskey.

Back then there wasn't any CCTV or any of the other modern tricks you find on properties today, those kinds of things were only for the elite. They were always aware of the risks, they knew how they could or couldn't be caught out, or so they thought.

They waltzed straight up to the guy in the field, acting all confused as though they'd lost their way and were looking for directions. As they approached, the second he glanced the other way, Bomf! One of the lads hit him with a straight right and knocked him for six. They quickly dragged him down to the house and out of sight to begin their interrogation on where the money could be found. They tied him up with some old rope they'd brought for the job to save them having to wrestle him during their interrogation.

"Where's the fuckin money?" One of them yelled.

Obviously no one wants to hurt anyone if they don't have to, tying him up was just to prove they meant business, nothing more, if they didn't need to hurt him then trust me, they wouldn't, but if they did, then so be it. This score would keep them in wages for a good few months, so it was worth taking a few risks.

"I haven't got no money, I haven't got none," Came his unconvincing reply.

They proceeded to rough him up a little more. He ended up with a broken arm, fractured face, battered, scratched and bruised. This went on for a while. They eventually came to the realisation that there really wasn't any money in the place, apart from a few hundred quid in an old jar, but not the spoils we'd been tipped off about. They'd broken his arm, smashed his face in, he was a stronger man than me if he did have the cash and to taken the pasting he did. But they had to come away with something, they'd already put their liberty at risk.

"Honest, Honest, there's no money, the only thing I've got is guns!" He pleaded.

Boom their eyes lit up. They hadn't come for guns, but they sure as hell were leaving with them, they'd be pushed to get more than a few grand for them but it was a score nonetheless. They had the contacts to move them.

Now when he said guns he wasn't kidding; apparently there were twelve in total, bullet rifles, shotguns and a decent selection at that. They rounded them up with all the ammo and any other accessories they could find, straps, nags, maintenance bits and pieces and the like and then promptly left.

Now that really is what took that particular crime it to the next level, commit robbery and the police are on the lookout, once guns are involved they're actively trying to hunt you down before another crime is committed. The police weren't going to leave this one alone. Not the CID, but the serious crime squad would be all over this one. There wasn't nearly as much gun crime back in 1984, so a blag like this stood out like a sore thumb.

At the time I was still staying at the hostel on Norfolk Park for three months, whilst I integrated back into society, as I'd only just got out of the nick from the seven and a half I'd been given off Judge Pickles. I knew it would be foolish getting involved in something like that the second I'd got out, I needed money, but it was too risky, I elected to give it a miss. That said, being hauled up in the hostel would have been a half decent alibi, but that one wasn't for me.

I don't know how it came back on them, there were no fingerprints, nothing physical in the way of evidence, and the team was tight. But somewhere much further down the line in the sale of the guns, someone had opened their mouth, and the trail led all the way back to the perpetrators. The police hadn't recovered any of the guns, but they knew who'd done it. Now I don't wish to dig up old ground, but I had a good inkling who'd dropped them in it. There were very few people who were aware of the guns being up for sale, and one of them was known for doing deals with the 'Rozzers' sprang, not one of the team, but a known fence, a latter day Fagin, a guy who would shift anything, but when it came to the crunch would buy his own freedom using the currency of information with the police. It was only a niggle, I didn't have enough to justify acting on those thoughts and tell the lads, but it did cross my mind.

Early one morning, while I was dead to the world in my hostel bedroom, sleeping sound knowing I'd done the right thing, a completely different story was unfolding for my pals.

05:30am. A tap on his shoulder. His eyes opened in a flash. He nearly jumped out of his skin. His first thought wasn't even the police he was that confident there was no trace of him on this one, more likely someone out for revenge or another crook looking for a quick sting. A copper was stood right over him with a gun at his nose, literally millimetres from touching his skin.

His arms were still under his pillow, apparently that's how he used to sleep.

The copper quietly said, "Take your arms from under the pillow slowly," You can image how it looked, they're looking for guns and he's sleeping with his arms under the pillow like a certified sniper.

It soon dawned on him it wasn't anyone else other than the police. It couldn't have been anyone else. They'd used the element of surprise to bring him in, not that they needed to, he wasn't going anywhere.

"What's it all abart?" He chelped.

"You'll see when we get down the Station." The armed copper replied.

Anyway they took him down to West Bar nick, like they had a thousand times before. The head copper's name was John Cannon. He was the gaffer of the serious crime squad and the one assigned to the case.

They took him down to the interview room, he's sat at the table and they threw an envelope at him.

He went "These are the people who are involved with you in this, open it!"

He opened it, two names, and they're right on the money, "We've got you and were looking for them now, care to tell us where they are?" Like fuck he did.

Next an officer from the Western Regional Crime Squad walked in with a shotgun in his hand and thrust it at him.

"Right, have you seen this before?"

He wasn't playing. It was a pathetic attempt to try and get his prints onto the weapon, the snakey little bastards! He hadn't trusted the police much before now, but that sealed the deal, never would he entertain them again.

It turned out by mid-morning his pals had already heard that he'd had his collar felt and they were already off and away.

So anyway, the coppers continued to grill him. Nothing was taped, it was all written down back then and then signed off. You had to read the statements back and make sure you weren't being stitched up. Once you'd signed, it was gospel.

His solicitor turned up, but he already knew evidence wise they were pretty tight, so he gave the obligatory "No comment" throughout the interview, giving away absolutely nothing. They knew him and his pals were involved but they just didn't have that edge to make it stick.

His solicitor came back a short while later and said, "They want you to go on an ID parade." The look on his face as though he had been one of the gang himself.

His heart sank, he was fucked. They'd not masked up and had spent a serious amount of time grilling the guy, he was done. It might sound stupid not 'ballying' up, but there were other properties around, potentially people passing by, they'd have had the law on their case before they'd even done anything if they'd have wandered around like a bunch of SAS through those fields. He'd already led his solicitor to believe he'd never been there, he had no reason to deter him from the line-out. He now had to put his money where his mouth was, he needed nothing short of a miracle now.

"Go for it, you weren't there, you'll be out in an hour." His solicitor said, if only you knew he thought.

Anyway he had to do it now. He headed down to the room where the ID parades took place. As he entered he nearly spat his teeth out, black guys, guys with long flowing ginger hair it seemed like in abundance, he stood out a mile, he was nothing like anyone else on the line-up, you couldn't make it up, he was royally being stitched up, I kid you not, they'd decided he wasn't getting away with this one, that was for sure. Back then he was clean shaven with short mousey hair, these guys were ginger, jet black, beards, tashes, glasses the lot. About twelve of them in total, it was like a game of 'Guess Who' on acid.

This wasn't like he'd seen in the movies, no one was hiding behind any glass, which is maybe where the miracle would come from, all face to face, maybe his bottle would go.

So he's stood in the line up, back then you had the option to take your shoes off, fuck knows why, he looked down and you can guess what was on his feet, the very same ones he'd had on, on that day.

"Right everybody, shoes off!" It seemed pointless but it was his only glimmer of hope. Adding to the confirmation of his guilt for any onlookers from the force.

Next minute, in walks the stocky little fucker, his old pal form the farm, the one he'd beaten black and blue, even broken his arm, he had no cause to help my pal out here, trust me. His arm was now in a sling, combined with a limp form the hiding he'd taken.

My pal's heart was going ten to the dozen, boom, boom, boom, boom, like you see in the cartoons beating out of their chest. Come on, fucking hurry up. He walks up and down two or three times, what the fuck is wrong with him, he must know it's him. He clocked him a couple of times, but his face never changed at all.

At the side of him was another kid, a lot smaller than him, blonde hair, he turned, pointed and said, "That's him thee're".

My pal's body frumped, every bone in his body let out a sigh of relief, I'm surprised he didn't slump to the floor. His solicitor game him the wink, the clever sod thinking I told you so. Well, it was sheer fluke, let me tell you.

In his brief return to the cell while they sorted the paperwork, John Cannon dropped by and said to him, "I fuckin know it's you, I fuckin know it's you."

What made him not pick my pal out? fear? I don't think so, he was a tough old sod, and he'd have to be pretty ruthless himself to point the finger at an innocent man. Was he stupid? Had the beating affected his memory? I can't imagine it was that bad. All I can say is, god bless you Mr Farmer for saving my pal, he owes you a pint (maybe more than one). That was possibly the luckiest day of my pal's life. It was done, none of them ended up getting fingered with that charge.

When he'd got out he went straight to his mate's house, one of the team, and said to his missus, "Where is he?"

She said, "He's fucked off"

He said, "Can you get in touch with him?"

She grabbed hold of him and went "Come here" and gave him a big kiss, she knew that if he was out, he was going to be OK. She managed to get hold of him in a boozer at the other side of Sheffield. He was straight round home and they celebrated like they'd just been released after a five year sentence, and I went over to join them. He'd only been in for the day, but there was no better buzz than getting off the hook from the law.

That was pretty much the last anyone heard on the subject. They knew, we knew, but we all knew it was going nowhere.

FATTORINI'S

'Burglary, 1985'

Don't be fooled by the chapter title; this wasn't another masked raid on big city jewellers, but an altogether different type of crime. Dave Lee was back on the scene and on the back of some gratefully received information he'd hatched a plan to burgle a wealthy Jewellery Shop owner's home in the Fulwood ward of Sheffield. You know the type, a high end established place, the type us Manor lads never had cause to visit.

The house was owned by the Fattorini family, the owners of a relatively high end jewellers in town. Fattorini & Sons was founded by Italian-speaking immigrant, Antonio Fattorini, in 1827. The firm's Sheffield shop had long been a familiar sight in the city centre. They were well revered in the industry so much so they'd been chosen to make the FA Challenge Cup trophy in 1911, hallmarking it in Sheffield. Bradford City FC got its name on the cup that year and if it was found on that particular expedition, I'm sure Wednesday's name would end up on there as well.

Like I'd mentioned earlier there was always an element of planning and it usually came about from a tip off of sorts, usually from another local villain. Information was a valuable commodity back then and the person supplying it was as valuable as any other member of the team. We always made sure they got their share. It might sound like you're giving away a lot there, but the jobs didn't exist without that kind of information, and if you didn't you weren't getting the next tip off, that's how it worked. The spoils this time were going to be well into four figures, we could afford to give a drink to whoever needed one, but that was Dave Lee's job to sort out, not mine, I was oblivious to where the information had come from and more than happy for it to remain that way.

We'd had some good information that there was some serious loot hidden somewhere in there and we were going to make sure we found it. Dave Lee has masterminded this one, I don't know where the information came from but he was certain there was a decent amount of cash and / or jewellery held within this particular property.

We'd sat in Dave's car and watched the house in the build up to this one for a good couple of weeks, seeing the comings and goings, working out when the place would be empty for longest and work out the most suitable time to get the job done, which turned out to be mid-morning, not as dark as we would have liked but on the plus side giving us good visibility and more than ample time if we didn't find what we were looking for straight away. Again CCTV was never a real consideration back then, we just had to keep the noise down and avoid being seen by any passersby.

Me and Dave Lee had sat in the car and cased the joint for weeks. Watching them leave for work, watching the maid arrive, watching her leave to go shopping, or so we assumed. I don't think Dave had any specific info. on what was in the house, but he'd said he knew where the owner lived. I don't know if it was his main residence or just one of many, but it looked the part and convinced me the job was a goer.

I was young, itching to do the job, but Dave showed me the right way to go about things. He had a PHD in crime. He convinced me it was important to keep your head, to learn the comings and goings, what kind of time window we had to get the job done. I was young, bored senseless and beginning to get more restless each time we turned up, but as the saying goes "Slowly, slowly, catchy monkey," and Dave was right usually right.

* * * *

Unfortunately things didn't really pan out for me on that one, and in some ways I was glad, because it wouldn't be long before I was hauled in again for a series of burglaries and that 'little one' wouldn't have helped. Instead Dave Lee had pulled another land in to help with the job, probably one that worked for a smaller cut or naïve to the risks. When it came down to it I sat that one out and by the sounds of it had a lucky escape, the kid who'd gone along with him got caught out, I was grateful that it hadn't been me. He told me the story of how that particular expedition had gone and ultimately how it had gone wrong. Here is what he told me:

One morning, they'd gone to do another one of their reccies, when Dave sprung it on him "It's today son."

His jaw dropped. He thought they'd just come to make mental notes again. "We're doing it now." He reinforced.

He didn't need to say another word. It was only 10am, The kid casually walked up the path whilst Dave waited in the car, key still in the ignition in case he needed to leave, sharpish.

The lad had managed to get in through a small side window and made his way to the front door, opened it and gave Dave Lee the signal. By Dave's estimation they had a full hour until the maid got back from shopping and wondered up the patch with her bags in tow. There wasn't even an alarm on the place, it should have been easy pickings for them.

Once they were both inside they searched the place top to bottom. There were a few valuables dotted about, but not the cold hard cash or expensive types of items they'd come looking for, cumbersome ornaments and paintings, ones that would take too long to shift, in every sense.

They searched high and low, things were starting to look like a waste of time. Not a sign of even a small cash box, never mind a decent sized safe, the type you'd expect to find in a well-to-do jewellers home, but Dave knew it was there somewhere, he could feel it in his blood.

They must have been in there half an hour, much longer and they'd be pushing their luck.

Dave kept saying, "I know there's something here." He just wouldn't give in.

It was becoming frustrating, the kid had removed his gloves and scratched his head, almost Stan Laurel like, the stress was getting to him and irritating his skin.

"I think we've fucked it Dave," He said.

As they were heading for the front door, about to leave with only a few hundred quids worth of what you'd call loose change and valuables the kid clocked it.

JACKPOT! Cleverly disguised as a side table, a cloth over the top of it and lamp on top, it just didn't look right and it wasn't. It was a safe, the safe they'd been looking for, a seriously heavy duty one at that, the kind they'd come to find, exactly as they'd pictured it, one that would be a pain to get into the motor, but worth every minute of the struggle.

They bundled it down the drive and back to the car in an epic struggle and headed straight back to base. It was heavy as hell. They'd two man lifted it into the boot, above knee height and 200lb. It went in the back of the Ford Capri and the suspension showed its pain.

They drove the safe across town to Dave's house, the excess weight noticeable to any onlookers. Once they'd got it back, eager as they were, they had all the time in the world to crack it. They were in two minds as to whether to draft in an experienced Peter Blower like Davy Dunford but decided against it and it took them a good couple of hours to prize it open, there was no intricate listening devices or keen ear involved, just brute force. It wasn't the type of thing you could pick up down the Argos, it was a real lump of Sheffield Steel, forged without expense in mind. If they could have opened it without damaging it they'd have been able to sell that as well, though by the time they'd finished with it that lump was good for nothing other than weighing in.

From that job they'd scored £16,000 worth of jewellery and £8,000 in cash after fencing the gear through one of their more trusted connections, You have to remember this was some time ago, a lot more by today's standards and with only the kid and Dave Lee to split it, they were more than happy with the result.

Money was no object for a man, or kid, of humble lifestyle like his back then after that generous score.

They'd pulled off a SEEMINGLY faultless job, though it would be one that would later come back to haunt them and it wouldn't be long before they were in the dock.

* * * *

Anyway, even though I'd sat that one out it wasn't too long before the knock came again for me aswell. Dave Lee and the kid in question had been pulled in for that particular burglary, associations were made and I was hauled in for other crimes. The police had linked together a few components of numerous crimes, mostly burglaries and I was in back in the frame.

We'd always been careful not to leave any prints on the jobs we'd been on, if we'd been eye-balled we'd have been pulled in well before now.

They'd pulled me and Dave Lee on the same day, and hopefully we'd be sent to the same nick together to help pass the time. That was rarely the case, but stranger things have happened.

For those little misdemeanours I was up in front of Chicken Neck aka Judge Michael Walker, another nemesis of mine, forever there to greet me when things came to a head.

"How do you explain your fingerprints being found at the victim's home?" Bellowed old Chicken Neck, playing Judge, Barrister and Executioner all rolled into one.

"The victim has confirmed that to their knowledge you have never been on their premises" He continued.

I'd always been so thorough. I couldn't work it out for the life of me. Then I remembered the story the kid had told me, *he'd momentarily removed his gloves and scratched his head, almost cartoon like, the stress had gotten to him and had irritated his skin. He'd put his hand down momentarily on what looked like a table cloth and felt something solid, Jackpot he'd thought. He'd jumped back and held his balance placing his hand on the wall.* All I could think was that at some point I must have done something very similar.

A momentary lapse of concentration during a couple of seconds of frustration had most likely cost me dearly, just like him. I had no explanation or retort to offer. They had me bang to rights with those prints and a guilty plea was all I could come back with

My partner in crime Dave Lee hadn't even worn gloves on most jobs, he'd once burnt away his fingerprints using some form of caustic acid, I think, all for the good of his criminal career, little did he realise they'd slowly redeveloped and were still recognisable to the police database and he was caught out in the same manner. If that wasn't dedication to being a crook then I don't know what is.

I went 'guilty' on a number of burglaries to avoid what would have been a certain six stretch. I was sentenced with Dave Lee and got four and a half years and he got exactly the same. Normally you wouldn't have got that amount of time, but I'd only just got out and clearly not learned any lessons inside.

We both got four and a half years, taking into account our previous criminal histories and blatant lack of regard to the law.

My first stop on that stint would be Armley, but this time in the mister's gaol, not the sugar coated YP Wing I'd visited on my way to Swinfen Hall.

BACK IN ARMLEY

'Eighteen Months, 1985'

Leeds Prison has played host to some well known guests over the years; Roy Chubby Brown; Charles Peace; John Poulson; Lilian Lenton; Charles Bronson; Stefan Ivan Kiszko; Peter Sutcliffe; Adam Johnson (the footballer), to name but a few, but make no mistake Armley is not a pretend prison for celebrities it has to be the toughest of all the prisons I'd stayed in, including Wakefield.

Jail today is nothing like it used to be, you have a television, a kettle, a toilet, most likely a burner phone fetched in up your best pal's arse. You have no reason to want to leave your cell, unless you're inclined to go to the gym, even that costs you thirty quid a month on the out.

When I went to jail they gave you a piss pot and a bible, that was your lot. I'd have hated to have a phone in prison; imagine phoning your missus at two in the morning when you're feeling low or you've just lost track of time and there's no one in, she doesn't answer, what thoughts must that send through a man's head?

Jail doesn't even come across as a punishment to the kids today. I didn't shy away from it, but it was still deemed a punishment back then. Twenty three hour bang up, any sign of rain and you were going nowhere.

One day in Armley me and a good mate Kenny Revel ended up down the block just because we were late coming out of a visit, and it wasn't even our fault. We got sent down the block for seven days and over Christmas and for no real reason, fucking ridiculous. The screws tell you when visits are up, so how's that make any sense? If you're face didn't fit you were in for a hard time in Leeds and even worse if the screw had gotten out of the wrong side of the bed that morning.

Maybe it's what's needed today, but they did go over the top a little back then. There were some real tough screws in Armley; the likes of Scarface Walker and Bootsy Walker, to name just a couple, to clarify they weren't related..

Bootsy Walker had a chain fed through his belt loop and then a link that lead into his pocket. Threaded onto it must have been about a hundred gold rings that he'd taken from various cons at numerous stages, parading around with them as trophies of the prisoners he'd conquered, that thing must have been worth a fuckin fortune. If you did anything, or even looked like you were going to, he'd drag you in and along with two or three other screws give you a good hiding, it was his way of keeping things under control and in the main it worked.

Walker was a prick and a bully, not necessarily as tough as the image I've just portrayed, but the screws had authority and outnumbered you in Armley, they'd be on you like a pack of hyenas if you stepped out of line. You could fight back, but you would never win. Ultimately, they punished you even worse for fighting back so you just took what was dished out and got on with things. People have died in gaol from beatings at the hands of screws and they've gotten away with it, just like in the country's police cells; that's a fact! And I didn't want to become one of those tragic cases.

Being friends with Paul Sykes on the inside usually came with a few perks, especially in Armley, and he was in during my second stint as well. We used to train a lot in the prison gyms, in truth there isn't much else to do in those places, you wouldn't find me down the gym generally 'on the out'. You could only go to the gym twice a week, but once I became pals with Paul, I was down there twice a day. I benefited greatly, I learned a lot from him and kept myself in good shape for anything that prison life might throw at me.

Paul wasn't given special treatment officially, the screws just used it as a way to make their own lives easier. If he was bench pressing dead weights down the gym then he wasn't bench pressing cons when he came back on the Wing. If he came back from the gym knackered, he wouldn't have the energy to be causing problems, that was the screws train of thought, though he often found the energy to cause a few. Paul was a one off and those kinds of tactics didn't always work .

Paul was always up early and used to be at my cell door at eight o'clock sharp every morning. He used to walk in with his chessboard and we used to play for an hour or so. We even used to leave the door open and the screws would join in as well.

"You alright, lads?" They'd ask. I'd have never got that kind of treatment if it wasn't for him.

The gym became my saviour. I took to it like a duck to water, being quick on the field, I already had big powerful legs, huge and strong, a natural athlete, which is a massive advantage in the likes of power lifting, I was off to a good start there.

Brian Nicholson one of the head screws in Armley asked me to stand in one day for a competition, as the resident Power lifter had been called out to attend his dad's funeral. I'd never really squatted before, I'd done a bit of dead lifting and bench pressing, but no real power lifting. I was there only to get the total in, make up the numbers so to speak.

Without ever doing it before, I stepped up and my natural squat was 160 kilos, my natural dead lift 220 kilos. Nicholson turned and said to me "If you carry on doing this you're gonna be making the prison team by the end of the week".

Within 6 weeks I was squatting 200 kilos and from then on I was entered into all the prison competitions. I did a lot Power lifting at both Wakefield and Leeds gaols. In prison though I'd gotten into the weights, I was a footballer more than anything, but in places like Leeds nick, there wasn't any football field, Walton was an exception. Armley was just one big exercise yard, if you want. We used to put benches up and use them as goal posts. Training in the gym was our only relief from the tedium of being banged up.

As 'payback' for helping Paul with his power lifting in return, but only on a couple of occasions I had to help him out with his Boxing training. Now I can take a dig but there are levels, and Paul knew it wasn't really my thing. He'd have a laugh with me, dig me in the ribs just that little bit too hard. When I was sparring with him I'd say "No hitting in the face" and every now and then he'd fucking clout me right around the swede, you know, not hard, but just enough so I knew about it, make my brain crackle. He'd catch me in the face and then apologise straight away, but he'd meant to do it, I could see it in his smirk, just messing about but I knew he'd be doing it again before long. I can't knock him, you can't go swimming without getting wet, as Frank Warren would say.

* * * *

Another time in Leeds nick, there was this little angry guy by the name of Freddie Mills from Newcastle, you may have heard of him. He was a little hard-core, always in trouble, and he hated Sykesy. Every time they crossed paths they used to fight, even though he was only a small guy he never backed down. He was a stocky little fucker though and when you looked at him, deep into in his eyes, they used to fucking shake, literally reverberate in his head and you'd think, fucking hell, he must be schizophrenic or some type of fucking mental.

Anyway we were in the canteen queue one day and they met, Paul and Freddie Mills, and they started fighting just like a bell had rung for round one, completely out of nowhere all hell broke loose.

A big fat Prison Officer (PO), Jack they called him, a big fat cunt came running in with a load of screws and somehow managed to stop them.

After the situation had diffused Jack the fat PO went, "Paul, you know where you've got to go, don't you?" Praying Paul was ready to play ball.

Paul went, "Yes, but I want payin first," A fair demand he thought.

"Right, get in the queue." He replied reluctantly.

I'm stood there fucking three behind Paul in the queue and as he's walked in, the screw at the back of counter said, "What's your number?"

"G82777" Giving out a little laugh.

The guy looked down at his pay log and said "He's already been paid." He obviously didn't know who Paul was and how things worked.

Jack the fat PO simply went, "Well, fucking pay him again then," And he did. The way he ruled that place in his prime was unreal.

Little things. Paul's cell in Armley was always directly at the side of these spiral stairs, ones which were reserved for the screws only. Instead of him walking right to the end of the landing and up and along like every other con, he always walked up these spiral stairs, usually with a screw shouting, "Sykes, who said you can walk up them stairs?" But this happened day in day out. They said it because it was their job, in reality it meant nothing.

He always went, "Them fuckers." Directing his glance in the direction of another screw and laughed as he blatantly ignored them.

Just little things like that, but nobody was willing to deal with him, and in general Armley was strict.

*   *   *   *

One day we, me and some of the lads, were in my cell doing prison tattoos, again this was only to pass the time of day, we weren't exactly operating in sterile conditions or even using the right utensils .

This young kid from Barnsley came into our cell. I asked him how long he was doing and he went "Six". I wandered what the fuck this young kid could have done to earn himself six years in the shovel.

"Six days!" He clarified. I nearly wet myself, why did they fuckin bother.

I asked him if he wanted a tattoo doing and he said yes, so I asked him what he wanted

He goes "I'll have Barnsley FC on my back". Cheers pal.

We got him in position and I fannied about for a bit to make out I was putting some effort in and I etched 'Clyde Broughton – Sheffield' into his back. The poor bastard was only doing six days, but he now had a permanent reminder of his short stay at Armley.

He was a real thick cunt, a typical Barnsley lad, and we had a great six days winding him up. I'd got him to fill out a request for his 'Ice Cream Tokens' and hand it in to Bootsie Walker, probably the worst screw in Armley.

Walker hit the roof "Broughton! Come here" He knew I was behind it.

I wandered over he went "Nice one," Even the meanest screw in Armley had seen the funny side of that one, which was a very rare occasion, trust me.

SYKESY

'In every instance he was in the right'

I made some great friends on the inside, but none stood out so much as the infamous Paul Sykes. On the inside I'd first met Sykesy in Armley as a YP on route to Swinfen Hall. On the outside it had been in the Springwood pub in Sheffield as a nipper. I'd made a point of keeping in contact with Paul when my sentences were over and our friendship blossomed, whether in or out of the nick we always kept in touch.

There are many stories, many rumours and many of them in my opinion just ammunition to ruin the reputation and memory of a man they couldn't control - The Hardest man in Britain, in my opinion. I've heard them all, but let me tell you from the Hawk's mouth, a lot of it is bollocks.

I have so many little stories about Paul it's been difficult to fit them all in to my story. Many I witnessed with my own eyes and others were relayed to me by trusted associates, who'd either worked with him or done time with him, but in the main they were from Dave Lee and another of Paul's close friends Davy Dunford. I never had any reason to doubt that there validity.

In the nick Paul was one of those people who liked things just so, he didn't listen to loud music or anything like that. He'd have Radio 5 on in his cell most days and he'd listen to things likes '*In Parliament*', academic programmes and the like, he was self educating all the time.

Anyway there was a strict rule enforced by the screws in Leeds nick where you had to turn your radio off by ten o'clock at night or it was confiscated. Paul was good with rules, yes he liked to break them, but so long as he knew what they were he was fine and he'd often urge others to abide by them, for what reason I never really worked it out, routine I guessed, but he always quoting them.

So one night this kid on the wing still had his radio on at well gone eleven o'clock at night, the screws had gone to rest and this kid was blaring out the obnoxious kind of music and radio broadcasting that Paul despised, the stuff be believed would rot your brain.

Back then there were these little square windows in the cell, and Paul's got his head up to the window, "Turn that fucking radio off!" He bellowed down the wing.

The kid obviously knew that Paul couldn't possibly know exactly who'd got their radio on, so the kid starts slagging him off through his own little window.

"Shut up you fucking cunt," The kid was giving it to Paul, knowing he couldn't see who it was from his cell, I personally heard all this.

So the next morning, Paul has gone upstairs and smashed up every single radio on the landing above and at the same time apologised to each con in case it wasn't him who had given him lip the night previous, but nonetheless and no matter how they begged he smashed every last one just to be sure and not one of them put up a fight.

"I'm sorry if it ain't you, but if it is I fucking got you, you bastard." He smiled as the radio's exploded against the wall.

To top it off that same night, he'd taken a basketball from the gym back to his cell and bounced it repeatedly against the wall all night and I mean literally all night long to keep everybody on the Wing awake and I was one of them. He knew that he'd got one up and that the lad who'd been mouthing off the night before would likely get a kicking from his own friends for the incident after those repercussions.

The things he did, and nobody would or could say anything, not even the screws. He was a man of principle and had such a great sense of humour and he was very, very clever, because he used to act daft and do daft things people thought he was an idiot, but he was far from it.

I'd heard in another incident on the out he'd been walking down the street and took a dislike to what was blaring out of somebody's kitchen window on their wireless, so he's walked straight up the garden gate, into the strangers house, turned the radio off and carried on about his business. Now that would have been fine, no one was hurt, but the homeowner happened to be a copper and the whole affair appeared a bit more sinister that it had actually been, an act of intimidation so to speak, and Paul ended up getting time for it. Who would risk their liberty for a bit of fun like that? Only a mad man, but like I say make no mistake he was a very clever bloke.

* * * *

Not just the times I'd spent with Paul myself, but I'd heard so many stories from my mentor Dave Lee about what Paul had got up to in Hull nick. I ended up in Hull myself further down the line, but didn't get the opportunity to spend time with Paul there as he'd been put on a new experimental wing to try and reform the more serious offenders.

Some of the stories Dave told me from Hull were hilarious and others were downright terrifying, that man lived by his own laws, not even the screws would bother trying to keep him in check, it simply wasn't worth the hassle.

Paul had once been walking past the television in the association area and Charlie Richardson the notorious London gangster had shouted over to him, "Paul, turn the telly over."

So Paul's gone up to the Tele and turned it upside down and fucked off without even looking back. Half of the London Underworld were in there at the time and they all broke out in hysterics. Charlie knew to expect nothing less from Paul, they got on well so I heard.

That was just his humour. It wasn't an attempt to stick two fingers up to the Underworld, it didn't matter who you were, you were getting the same response. Whether in humour or in malice what can you say to him? Nothing, because he's fucking ruthless, it doesn't matter who you are or how you're connected, you can't deal with a man like that, so it's best not to bother.

Some of the best stories Dave Lee told me about Sykesy were from Hull nick. I wasn't there personally but Dave's word was as good as my own, he didn't need to make shit up to impress me, we'd grafted together got sent down together and were both good pals of Pauls.

Another tale involved the notorious Roy Shaw. It was Davy Dunford who told me that when Sykesy was in Hull nick ad at the point 'banging everybody'. The resident of the nick were a little relieved to hear the notorious Roy Shaw's was in his way, a champion in the unlicensed boxing game and a man who'd even fought Lenny McLean and any other credible name you could care to mention from London and all this.

To put pay to all the nonsense that surrounded them both guys agreed to get in the prison gym boxing ring and see how it went, there was no real malice, in fact I'm sure they both would have relished the opportunity to 'have a dig' with someone with an ounce of boxing skill.

Unfortunately that didn't last too longs, two punches later, Paul had knocked him spark out, a week or so later they went again and the outcome was almost identical. That put pay to that one. The northerners held the title.

Now that might sound a bit farfetched or a bit like gaol folklore nonsense, but I was to hook up with Roy Shaw many years later, and the response I got from him kind of confirmed what I'd been told. I didn't want to indignify Roy by asking directly, he was a great bloke by all accounts, but he came back with the perfect response but you'll have to read the final chapter to find that about out.

Another tale from Hull, told to me by Dave Lee, involved the infamous Charles Bronson, now known as Salvador. It turned out that Bronson was regularly picking on another con by the name of Fred Lowe. Fred was a guy, for whatever reason, who was never getting out. A bearded / spectacled weird looking type, he used to sit on the landing ripping newspapers up, roll by roll, just ripping them up into neat strips and laying them out, lord knows why, probably just going stir crazy. On a couple of occasions Bronson just went up to him, booted the strips of the landing balcony and grabbed any remaining papers and slung them aside.

So Sykes got wind of this. He took a chair and put it up against the wall close to where Fred used to sit. The next time Bronson motioned over towards the spot where Arthur used to sit, Paul set off and duly intervened. He had a quiet word in Bronson's ear and made him sit on the chair looking at the wall with his face only an inch from the wall, like a naughty school boy and told him in no uncertain terms, "If you give him any more shit I'm gonna fucking smash your face in." That was the end of that.

* * * *

Often when I was in the nick with Paul he would take the liberty of feeding himself. He'd wander along to the server and the kitchen lads behind the server would usually put their utensils down and let him get on with it. More often than not I'd be at the side of him because we'd just come back from gym, and whatever he'd put on his tray, he would put on mine as well.

One day there a big blonde-haired kid running the server who didn't want to play ball.

Paul said to him, "Are you gonna serve me or shall I serve myself?" A question that only really had one answer.

"I don't wanna get you in trouble," Paul continued with a wry smirk.

"You'll get the same as every fucker else." Said the kid, attempting to stand his ground, something he might later regret. I was praying he'd just keep his mouth shut, for his own sake. If he was clever enough he'd put his utensils down and let him get on with it.

So Paul went, "Alright, you win." And wandered off. He had to be playing a game I knew that couldn't possibly be the end of it.

That night me and Paul had been down the gym training, doing our weights as usual, when I saw all these white shirts come running past, kitchen lads who appeared to be running for their lives.

I knew exactly what was happening. I ran in the opposite direction to the white shirts and down towards the server. I could hear what could only be described as audible clouts coming from the kitchen.

When I got there Paul was walking out of the office and handed me a towel and said, "Go and give him that." And walked off

I walked into the kitchen and there he was, the big fat blond haired kid, laid out, and I'm not exaggerating, he was split him from the top of his head right to his nose end and his eyes were wide like they'd been propped open with matchsticks. I swear to god I thought he was fucking dead!

So put the towel over his nose and wondered what the fuck to do next. But lucky enough, a few moments later he did fucking wake up, my heart started to beat again.

All the kid had to do was put his fucking utensils down and let Paul feed himself and for that mistake he was placed an inch from death. Paul always had the last laugh if the argument could be won with violence, it was his way or the highway. In that particular incident Paul knocked his knuckle right up into his hand, but it came with the territory.

Food was always a big issue in the nick. It makes pure sense and like Paul said in his book Sweet Agony. Why is he getting fed the same to eat as someone who's only 'this big' and who is not even interested in training. A sixteen and a half, seventeen stone man needs more food than a nine, ten stone man, doesn't he? He simply has a bigger engine, but in the nick everyone gets the fucking same, don't they? Even the prison fucking cat! But Paul sorted that little problem as well.

*   *   *   *

Now a part of prison folklore, and re-born as a viral internet sensation for his crazy rants caught on camera by ITV's First Tuesday back in 1990, Paul was more than that and I can genuinely call him a friend, one I could call on no matter what.

I've seen him lock jails down and I reckon that's where all the bullshit stems from, the authorities used him, knowing that if other people were scared of him they didn't have to keep them under control themselves and that kind of thing. They used Sykes as a deterrent.

Paul was a friend of mine from the moment I met him, both in and out of the big house, sometimes mental, sometimes out of order, but always loyal. Rumours, rumours, all second hand nonsense. If you didn't know Paul then you never will know the man behind the myth.

Because of his awkward ways and unmanageable antics, he spent a lot of time down the block and on route 43, a place often reserved for the likes of sex offenders and people like that for their own safety. But he was there for a different reason. I'm sure that's probably where some of that bullshit comes. Believe me, if Sykesy had shagged any YPs in there, they wouldn't let that lie. They'd go and tell somebody and he'd get done for it, end of. As my good friend Delroy will tell you himself, if they were doing it, they were doing it of their own accord in 99% of instances, or for baccy.

Then main sentence where I spent a lot of time with Paul was in Armley. We were close pals in there and he was devastated when I was released. I can honestly say, he never and I mean never, ever, even once, threatened. Maybe I should feel a little honoured, but I was under no illusion he could be a fucking nightmare.

MONEY WITH MENACES

'1988'

The eighteen months I'd been served for the burglaries passed quickly, aided by the new found companionship I found in Sykesy and the extended gym hours, and other privileges, afforded by that friendship.

The year was 1987 and I'd been released once again from another stint in prison. Again regret was never an emotion that featured in my life at that time and if I'm honest I was back on the take within days of my release.

For a short period I made an attempt to work a straight number in Asbestos Removal. The wages were relatively good and I had opportunities to earn even more by contracting away, but it just never weighed up to me. I was earning seven hundred quid a week back then, which was damn good money for 1987 / 88 and topping up with the proceeds of one or two jobs on the side (crimes). But working away for extra money didn't really stack up to me, much to the disbelief of the other lads on the firm's books. There were always 'other ways' to top-up. I wasn't shy of a few quid at that time anyway, put it that way. I was making more by staying at home than I ever could working away.

As things panned out I didn't really need to work a straight number at all, but it always made a good baseline and helped when you needed to get the odd bit of finance, whether it be a car or house, without the supporting paperwork you were screwed, but as you read further on, there are ways to obtain that as well.

Fuck working, I preferred to graft, and in my world those two words had very different meanings. To this day my hands are still as smooth as the day I was born, not something to be proud of I guess, and not a boast you often hear in Sheffield, but such is life and it wouldn't pay for us all to be the same.

That period was a short stretch of normality for me, life was sweet, but never for long for old 'Broughts.' One day an opportunity presented itself, it seemed pretty straight forward, and the risks were low, again I was to prove myself wrong and walk straight into trouble.

A local guy owed a pal of mine twenty grand, straight business from the motor trade, no skulduggery, nothing untoward just a genuine business deal gone sour. These things often happen in straight business and very often get swept under the carpet as people give companies the run around, disappear, or go bust. The knock on effects are usually bad for all concerned and every now and then the bent world has to be drafted in to intervene, to create a form of justice that the straight world can't offer, if you know what I mean.

After a debtor had refused to pay on numerous occasions, my friend had asked me to intervene in return for half of the debt, it was half or nothing at all for him. Now if you don't get rumbled that has to be the easiest money you could ever earn, in most instances the debtor already knows they're in the wrong and going to the police is out of the question, even for them. I know half sounds generous, but what's half of nothing?

So I made my way over the guy's business premises. I went on my own, which was a little naïve, even if I'd only had back-up waiting around the corner it would have been something, if I was honest I hadn't really considered what I was letting myself in for.

I walked into the guy's office, sat down and we chatted amicably, he knew why I was there before I'd even opened my mouth and things were jovial initially. He was giving me the impression this would be an easy touch, but as time wore on it became clearer he thought he could fuck me off as well, he thought I was all mouth.

Going to his business premises, not his house, later turned out to be a BIG mistake. As the conversations prolonged, I realised things were going nowhere, so I lunged over the table, dragged him out into the yard, and began to bash the fuck out of him right there on his own premises. I eventually got through to him using my fists.

The 'hiding' had the desired effect and a couple of days later he stumped up the full balance of the cash that he owed to my friend and I got my dues, ten grand; not bad for an hour's work, a successful hour's work at that, or so it seemed at the time. Me and Wendy had a good weekend on the back of it and parked most of the money while we considered our options on investing it in something useful for the family.

* * * *

A week or so later, the incident was steadily falling to the back of my mind when things came to a head. I had my collar felt and found myself back in the interview room with my counterparts from CID. Their hatred for me was real by now, if they pulled me in I was most likely getting convicted, they wouldn't waste their energies on anything less.

They checked me over, my hands, no marks to be found, I made my excuses, "Nothing to do with me officer", but in the back of their minds they still had an ace up their sleeve, one which they were struggling to contain.

After some tactical to'ing and fro'ing that turned out to be a complete waste of my time, they rolled out that ace in the form of a TV and video cassette recorder, what the hell was going on now, they certainly weren't giving me a coffee break and the chance to catch up on last week's Corrie. The Detective pulled out a video tape, put it in the recorder, pressed play and on it came.

"Do you know who that guy is there?" He asked.

I squinted at the screen. My chin hit the floor; he looked very familiar, very familiar indeed. Unbeknownst to me the whole thing was caught on CCTV. This was 1988, yes there were cameras here and there but generally not, unlike now, it wasn't always a crooks first consideration, like it is now. Since that incident I still clock the cameras everywhere I go to this day, even if I go into a shop with a grand in my pocket and no bad intention, I scan the place, it's just force of habit.

I began to wonder why three weeks later, the incident had ticked over in the guys mind and he'd decided to contact the police. He'd cleared his debts but decided he wanted payback. He wasn't of a position to send anyone to fill me in, so he went to the law, he never even had to come to court the dirty little snake.

* * * *

My court date arrived. The circumstances surrounding those events being caught on camera was clearly against me, but the fact that the debtor was clearly a man of low moral values meant the judge was slightly more lenient with me than he might normally have been and some would say he was downright blasé towards the whole matter given my existing criminal record.

By the time I'd got out of that courtroom I was only given a suspended sentence, bound over for twelve months to behave myself, which was always tricky, but not completely out of the question.

It was agreed that I would spend twelve months on license and if I managed to behave myself I wouldn't see prison at all for that particular misdemeanour. I couldn't believe my luck.

The judge on that case had to be my favourite of them all, though funnily enough the only one who's name I cannot remember, getting off was never as memorable as getting sent down it would seem.

Funnily enough my good pal Sykey's got sent down for the exact same thing when he went to threaten a union official in Blackpool for a similar amount of money, strange little world we live in.

BRED FOR 'FEYTIN'

'My Butch'

This chapter might not sit well with everyone, including myself, but I feel I would be a fraud not to include it in my story. For a spell I'd gotten involved in the world of dog fighting through a friend of mine by the name of John Cook who lived in Halifax. I'd met him in Walton nick whilst I'd been on my first sentence, the seven and half.

John Cook was a half cast lad, a strong kid and a good power lifter. He was from Durham originally and had got five years when I'd met him in Walton. Someone had been intimidating him, so he'd gone round to the guy's house, knocked on the door and as he heard the guy coming down the stairs, which were directly in front of the door, he put a shotgun through the letter box and blasted it off straight into the guy's stomach. It could have been anyone, he didn't even look. Because the guy who he'd shot was a bit of a 'name' he'd had to fuck off, and that's how he ended up living in Halifax.

I'd arranged to go see him over in Halifax, not far from the town centre. He was living in one of those old town houses you often find in city centres, you know the really tall four storey ones, the type sometimes used as solicitor's offices. A place with a cellar and an attic, ideal for low key gatherings and that's where I'd first been exposed to the world of dog fighting.

I'd always been interested in animals and the outdoor pursuits, whether it be hawking, coursing etc. so dog fighting seemed no different in some respects, and if I'm honest I was instantly, but naively, drawn to it.

So a pal of mine who lives in Sheffield, who already had a fighting dog had told me there was a dog coming up for sale in Darlington, only ten months old, never done a thing in the fighting game, never even had a roll (that's a low level confrontation if you will, just to see if the dog is game, see if it was a quitter, a bit like sparring is as to Boxing).

I travelled over to Darlington and when I got there I had the choice of two dogs. One of them was a right big bastard, weighed about 75lbs stripped, absolutely solid, I was being swayed, it wasn't the dog I'd come to buy, but this one was an absolute beast and looked ten times the animal the other one was, though a little older.

The kid said to me "This dog would absolutely blitz the one you've come to buy," And I could believe it, it was naturally a lot bigger, older or not.

"But this younger one's got potential, he's only ten months old, you can train him yourself, no bad habits to sort out."

So I bought the ten month old and named him Butch. An American Pit Bull, they're outlawed now, but they weren't at the time. I paid five hundred quid for him back in 1990.

I'd already bought my treadmill, and everything else I needed to train my beast before I'd even bought the dog, I was ready to get him into training the moment he got home.

You can't teach a dog how to fight, you can't sit it down and say "Reyt when that's got hold of your neck you grab its leg", you can't talk tactics, the only thing you can do is keep it fit for the fight. It's like me or you entering a five mile race as you are now, you've got no chance, but if you train for a few months, then your chances improve, it was all about preparation. I got Butch fit on the treadmill, bulking him up on a raw meat diet, giving him a thirst for blood.

It also comes down to 'gameness', you have to buy the blood, just like buying any regular pedigree, you're buying into the breeding line, and that usually comes at a premium. In this game though a beautiful looking dog wasn't the right dog to buy, it had to have the inbuilt instinct to fight, and they do have it, trust me.

I'll never forget the first time I took him out, I let him off the lead and a minute later he'd already ran away from a Springer Spaniel, it chased him down the road and bit him on the arse, and he screamed like a fucking cat. I put my head in my hands and mumbled to myself *Oh my fuckin god. What have I done here* I thought, with the cost of the dog and the treadmill etc I had nearly a grand tied up in my prospect, good old Butch.

We carried on walking, and you see reactions in dogs, something struck me, a glimpse of his true inner self and I saw he was coming of rage, I knew there was more beyond that first incident, possibly a turning point for him, that little nip on his arse, had tainted him even. He would never run off again and woe betide anyone or anything that tried to put fear into him again, that little incident had done him the world of good, or for the fight game at least.

You could see in his eyes, the way he looked at other dogs, his ever changing personality, growing in confidence, he was now a completely different dog. We were out again on the Manor fields just a few weeks later and a Labrador came over, showing aggression, and he was on it, obviously I was there and managed to pull him off, but it was an example of how his mindset had changed, it didn't matter if it was a Labrador or a Tiger, he wasn't backing down, I knew for certain now his bubble had burst and it was time to up the training regime.

To get started I'd rolled him against a guy who'd paid four hundred pound for his dog, the money he'd spent on his dog was supposed to be going towards his wedding, the dog was an investment, a lame attempt to double his money, let's just say even never ended up getting married.

His dog was supposed to be the business, but after twenty minutes it quit, he ended up shooting the poor bastard, he was devastated, it had cost him his marriage. I never understood that mentality, I was training my dog to fight and I loved him, if he'd fallen at the first hurdle I'd have taken him home and continued to look after him like a son.

To be honest for a dog to give up after twenty minutes, that was meant to be good, he clearly hadn't conditioned or trained it right. I've seen fights go on for as long as an hour and ten minutes and that was my own dog, and he came away with only a couple of scratches, not literally, but point deductions if you will, for bad behaviour e.g. if my dog grabbed hold of his bollocks, you don't want them ripping each other's balls off, it's not good for maintaining the blood line. In those situations they split em up, the owners each drag their dogs back to their corners and then because my dog had the advantage he has to hold his back while I release mine and let it run over and slam it before the fight can continue, so he regains advantage.

Butch was eighteen months old when he'd had his first real fight, in fact he only had two fights in total. One in a cellar in Halifax against a dog called Midnight for twelve hundred quid, I knew Butch wouldn't have any problem with that one, he was a beast, catch weight as well, dead on 54lb, so he could have fought a dog anywhere up to 65lb. Once you tipped 50lb, weights went out of the window, you were into the realms of super heavyweight if you like.

One night I'd come home pissed, when I lived down the bottom end of Wybourn. I'd taken Butch out for a walk and we'd headed down to this big cow field, there were about thirty beasts all stood at the fence and the dog is pulling 'n' snarling, I just let him go, *BOMF!* He was straight in. I climbed the fence and got in myself and I could hear the commotion all the cows were gathered around this one cow, the biggest of the lot, Huawwwrrr! Huawwrrr! Making primeval noises. When I got up close I could see the fucking dog was latched onto its nose, just like a lion when it suffocates its prey, how could a cow carry that weight on the end of its snout for that long, 50lb of dog, probably more as he was out of training, more like 60lb. How could a dog weighing 60lb bring down and kill a beast that probably weighed 800lb, but it did. Eventually after running round the field, struggling to breath that 50lb is gonna eventually feel like two ton.

I'd managed to get him off, but it did die, probably the strain and some element of shock combined had killed it. Freddie Bonzo aka Fat Freddie, the enabler I mentioned earlier, who hung out in the Springwood ended up with the cow, and sold it off for dog meat.

My venture into that sport didn't last too long, eventually I got another two and a half years behind bars, for which I ended up doing twenty months, which was a long time for a dog to be out of the game, close to fifteen years in human terms. By the time I'd come out my fighting machine was no more than a family pet, roughly four and half years old and lovingly over fed by my missus Wendy. Once a catch weight, two time winner, he was now a portly beast laid by the fire. As a two time winner, one more fight and he'd have been a champion in the fighting ring, but the law always came knocking.

The second fight had been in Maltby against a Swamper Dog, that's just a breed, I don't recall the dog's name, again Butch won without problem. I won't dwell on the in's and outs of the fight. Experience is usually a teller, if the dog has done it before and knows the script, it's not gonna burn itself out in the first five minutes.

I later bought another Pitbull, a bitch, this time from John Cook in Halifax. It was bred from a Grand Champion by the name of Black Jack Bronson from up North and a bitch by the name of Bourgeoisie. This wasn't long before the ban came in, you could keep your dog but you had to have it neutered and assessed, I refused to do that. I'd already had the letter telling me I had to have the dogs 'done 'in the next four weeks. If I didn't comply they were gonna come and if I didn't play ball they'd be shot.

One morning I was still laid in bed and the armed police turned up with the RSPCA, I'd heard the knock., I knew why they were here and armed to the hilt for my poor dog. With hindsight I wished I'd have had them done now, they were good dogs and they deserved better for everything they'd done for me, they'd have had their retirement in front of the fire to look forward to, but I knew I'd let the clock tick for too long, the police wouldn't be going back on this one, it's not often they get chance to fire those guns. I loved my dogs, I couldn't even bring myself to go down, I just stayed in bed. Our lass went down and there they were all tooled up

I've had lots of dogs, lots of working breeds Whippets, a Cane Corso called Spike (without the cropped ears, something they do to make them look more menacing, one of the first in the country). The Cane Corso is the ultimate guard dog, you don't even need to teach them, it's in their blood.

I've keep all manner of species, not just dogs, Harris Hawks, Owls all 'workers', trained to do what is in their blood, everyone has their view but no one can tell me I didn't love those animals. The cruel part when you've got a dog that can fight, that loves to fight, the real cruel part is taking the dog to the fight, but once he's there he loves it. When my dog was getting battered I've never seen his tail wag so much, even when in grip, it would still be going, looking for his chance to get back on top, watch dogs play fighting, you'll see exactly what I mean.

In all these underground sports there are rules, it's down to the owner to know when to call it a day, it's down to me to take my animal out when I know it's had enough, that's usually when the fight ends.

In Dog fighting, most people that do it love their animals, their prize possessions, when your boy has had enough you throw the towel in and save him. I've never seen a dog killed in any of the fights I attended, I'm not saying it hasn't happened, I'm sure it has, but it's not completely how you'd be led to believe.

There letting it do what it wants to do? My current dog wants to catch Hares, you're not even allowed to do that now. I would never stop that in the same way the Jack Russell wants to shake a rat to death, you don't tell it to do that, it's in its history.

Even though Staffys have a reputation and are tough, they're not game like a PitBull is, it's in the blood, a Pitbull should not be allowed as a pet, they're monsters, the one I had, if I was walking down the road and there was a full grown male tiger, my dog would jump in its gob in a heartbeat and commit suicide in the name of being game.

THE HORSE & LION

'Screwed over by Judge'

A short time later another incident occurred, one somewhat out of my control and one that resulted in another stint behind bars.

The 'money with menaces' incident was done and quickly fading into the background. It was water under the bridge in my eyes, but I still had twelve months to do on license.

I'd learnt another valuable lesson there, not to underestimate the rise of technology in particular the dawn of CCTV and had every intention of keeping my nose clean. I'd hate to be a criminal these days, the odds are very firmly stacked against you, compared to the good old days of cops 'n' robbers.

I'd been placed on a suspended sentence for twelve months. I never really viewed it as a problem, in the scheme of things it wasn't a long time to keep myself out of trouble. Yes, I still needed to earn, but bad fortune would ensure it wasn't long before I was back inside, and that's without any criminal intent, just a badly timed incident down one of my local boozers and a little helping hand from another nemesis of mine Judge Lawrenson.

The incident in question took place at the Horse & Lion Pub situated on Park Grange Road. The same pub that featured in the video for the Arctic Monkeys' 2006 number one hit 'When the Sun Goes Down'. It's now joined the ever growing list of pubs in the Sheffield graveyard for licensed premises and has been converted into a convenience store. The incident itself was a minor issue that somehow got way out of hand and ended up with me back inside.

At the time I had my prize Pit-Bull, Butch by my side. We'd just been to a local dog show and had gone back to the Horse & Lion for a few beers. Stood by the bar with my dog and the missus by my side, we'd had a good day and were celebrating our second place, any excuse for a pint, I'd still have been celebrating if we'd come last or the car had broken down on the way there.

My boy could be a bit lively, but he always right by my side and well under control, he always brought a lot of attention wherever we went.

While I'm stood at the bar a woman came over to the juke box beside me. She'd just dropped a couple of twenty pence pieces into the machine, when I turned and jokingly said, 'The dog likes Simple Minds?'

Her face gave the impression I'd just called her a washed up old slag. I'd never seen this woman before in my life, to say she took it the wrong way was somewhat of an understatement. She'd thought that little joke had been a genuine slant on her intelligence, with hindsight the dog was right, how she had the ability to operate that machine I'll never know.

She turned around, got right up in my face and told me in no uncertain terms to "Fuck off."

She was so close up in my space I'm surprised Butch didn't take her leg off there and then, they have an instinct in those types of situations, and are known take their music seriously.

So I calmly said "Who do you think you're talking to, you silly bastard?" Further helping to diffuse the matter, as you can imagine.

To set the scene, I've got my dog in one hand and my pint still in the other, somewhat restricted but aware of my situation enough to know I needed to be ready for if and when, things went wrong.

She was no less than a foot in front of me, when she erupted, a puff of steam came out of her ears as an early indicator and then she went to slap me.

Instinct quickly took over, my hands still full I lifted my arm to block the attack, a natural reaction in that kind of scenario but fuckin disaster struck, the glass caught her on the cheek, oh dear, *Here we go again Clyde* I thought! Whatever had happened, however it had come about, whoever's fault it was, I knew I'd be taking the fall for it.

Even in her statement it said we were in a 'close proximity / face to face situation of about a foot', what could I do? Nothing but a little nick on her ugly face, she'd been cut, not 'glassed' in the traditional sense, if there is such a thing, she was the aggressor, but I was Clyde Broughton and this was only going to go one way and it wasn't mine.

If I'd thrown a real move at her with that glass in my hand she'd have been disfigured for life, put to sleep on the spot, but that wasn't how it happened, for the record, I couldn't have got out of the way even if I'd wanted to.

Now this isn't really the type of crime that makes for good reading, but it happened.

As it turned out, even though she'd been glassed I was the one that ended up getting stitched up... during sentencing!

*   *   *   *

After a short spell on remand I was back in the local magistrates' court again. Contrary to the initial advice from my barrister I was determined to go 'Not guilty', after all I wasn't guilty, but come dinner time the story had been spun and my Barrister approached me to reiterate that advice.

"Clyde, I'll advise you now, you need to go guilty on this one." Was he fucking joking.

My face hit the floor, we both knew the score, in a just world I should never have had to plead guilty but in my own best interest, but I now had no other option.

"Lawrenson is willing to do a deal. If you don't you're gonna get 5 or 6 years, but he's willing to do a deal".

A deal, I didn't know the terms but the word 'deal' was a welcome sound to my ears. Sure, it wasn't fair but it was damage limitation time. I'd already been on remand in Leeds for a couple of few months prior to the trial, I had a good feeling about the outcome.

I said "Tell him I'll accept 18 months for a guilty plea" Like I was in a position to call the shots. I'd be saving the judge the hassle of deliberation and a couple of day's courts costs, which always featured heavily in their thinking, the cleverer ones anyway.

Dirty bastards had me over a barrel, but like I said it was damage limitation time. So my barrister went back up and shortly after they shouted me up. As I entered the room he gave me a little thumbs up.

Get in! I thought, 18 months, back then you didn't do half remission, you'd do 12 months, with 8 months already behind me on remand in Leeds that left me with not much left to do at all.

The jury got sent out, I was asked how do you plead, I said "Guilty", thinking I'd got the deal done.

A few high brow criminal justice discussions went off behind the scenes, formalities were approved and the judge emerged from his chambers to make sentence.

The judge had returned and proclaimed "I sentence you to 18 months in prison Mr Broughton …. " My face lit up.

"But you're already on license in the form of a twelve month suspended sentence. Therefore that will also come into play, hence making you're term two and a half years in total." My mind went to mush and my heart nearly stopped, I'd been done up like a fucking kipper.

What the fuck! I'd been led well and truly led up the garden path, how did I even forget myself about the twelve month bender, I hadn't really, a deal was a deal in my book, but I vowed never to do a deal with the justice system again.

So, from what I'd thought was going to be eight months, from what I guessed, there would be another four, I ended up doing twenty months in reality. They'd well and truly fitted me up and I was on my way back to the Shovel! Self defence is a terrible thing.

Even as a criminal I'd always had a healthy respect for the law and the upholding of justice, but that incident tainted me to this country's justice system and to boot I've never been a big fan of Simple Minds since that day.

LINDHOLME

'1988 Prison Wedding (and the riots)'

My next stop was 'HM Prison Lindholme, a Category C/D men's prison located near Hatfield in neighbouring Doncaster, South Yorkshire. It only opened in 1985 and houses approx. 1,005 inmates.

Lindholme was one of the more watered down nicks, in my opinion. You could move from dormitory to dormitory, they weren't gated, so you could wander around the prison and visit your friends as you pleased. Don't get me wrong it's a real prison, but as a Cat C/D they're not expecting the kind of trouble that comes with the higher category prisoners, or calibre of criminal.

One particular night me and a couple of my pals were sat around, doing what we always did, playing Chess, having a game of cards, just generally having the crack, not literally I might add, though it was available.

The next minute two guys walked in with pillow cases over their heads with the eyes cut out, like a couple of Klan members and both tooled up with bed legs in their hands.

"Right lads were having a riot" The bigger one stated.

"You're either with us or you're not!" They added, in unison.

"Come with us or stay here, but things are about to go off." The other smaller one continued.

"We'll give it a miss if that's alright" I replied as though he'd merely offered me a cuppa.

Seconds later it all just kicked off. I'd have loved to have joined in, if only for the adrenalin, but I was on a short sentence and wanted out, I chose not to get involved. Me and the members of my little chess club just sat back and watched the screws take a beating and the nick getting trashed, whilst we played the petrified onlookers. This one went on for most of the night until the Burglars (riot police, screws with batons, shields, dogs etc.) came in and got the place back under control.

When things had calmed down a little, and with the prison back under control we were all ushered down to the visiting room, an area that made a better base / point of control for the lads trying to take over the prison.

It was all a big game. When we'd got down there, two of the lads, pals of mine, Brian Weyland and Brian Favin had removed the pillow cases from their heads to make any unsuspecting screw think that they'd never been involved. Five minutes prior, and still masked up, they'd gone and raided the dispensary of all the drugs as well as the canteen of any tobacco.

We all sat there waiting for things to completely calm down so that we could go back to our rooms and get some sleep, the day's events had really taken it out of us, but we had to wait for the nod from the screws before we could return to our cells. The whole nick had been trashed, the damage ran in the millions I reckoned.

Any way I was sat in the visiting room with my pillow case with all my worldly possessions in it and one of the Brians came up to me and gave me a whole load of Baccy and Diazepam, Wobbly Eggs, Valium, the lot, you name it, if it was available in that prison it was in my pillow case.

As I'd been one of the first in the visiting room and seen by the screws they had no reason to check me, whilst others were getting their contraband taken I just waltzed back to my room with my pillow case fully stocked with goodies. I didn't need any tobacco for about four months after that, not bad going for someone who'd kept out of the chaos and come away with a clean sheet.

I kept most of it buried out in the gardens in the area where I worked, nipping back whenever I needed, whether it be for myself or to make a couple of quid to retrieve my contraband.

I was in Lindholme for two of the main riots. Almost identical scenarios, the lads wanted a bit of fun, Lindholme wasn't a harsh environment like Armley or Wakefield. In both instances by the time the screws could react the damage was already done. I never got myself involved, there's only ever one winner in there, so I just used to sit back and revel in it and pick up the odd bonus.

By sheer good fortune the two Brian's went straight under the radar as well, they were as innocent as me in the eyes of the screws. There was never any real protest about the conditions or a valid cause, just a bit of fun and an opportunity to raid the coffers. A few of the lads even got over the fence, it wasn't long before they were back though, the chaos made a good distraction for an escape. I think this about 1988/1989.

*   *   *   *

There was one positive that came during my time at Lindholme, one that made that stint much more bearable, I married my fiancé Wendy whilst still in that place. Not the most romantic of scenes I know.

While I was banged up in Lindholme my missus Wendy had been left waiting for me once again, why she tolerated it I do not know, everyone loves a bad boy I guess, but I was testing her resilience to breaking point by now, I'm sure.

Back in those days if you got sentenced to more than twelve months they took your house away from you, unless, of course, you were married. It wasn't that I didn't want to marry Wendy, trust me, she is and always has been the love of my life and the mother of my children, we just had to make it happen a bit sharpish, for both our sakes.

I'd learnt of the twelve month housing loophole from an old friend, no other than Scarface Walker, the old bastard of a screw from Leeds nick. He'd told me that if I got married Wendy could keep the house on, so we decided to get married as soon as we could and do it in true prison fashion.

Whilst I was inside I was only ever got let out on a few very rare occasions. It was usually only allowed for family reasons, my father's funeral being one of them, but you were always accompanied by a screw.

After some persuasion I'd been sanctioned by the Governor to be let out to get married, the year was 1988, and it I was still hauled up in Lindholme. They'd agreed to let me out for half a day accompanied by a screw, and at a cost to us of a hundred and twenty quid, imagine paying that to get married these days, but we had our shotgun wedding and we were happy.

We rocked up at Doncaster Registry office to carry out the formalities. Wendy turned up, beautiful as always, sat in the back of Wally Cooper's Ford escort car, done up in the usual wedding styling, a real dingle wedding. The paperwork was signed and then we were headed off to the Prison Chapel (Church) at Lindholme for a more traditional ceremony. I must be the only con in Lindholme Nick who's had his leg over in the church. It was a precious short time, a necessity to keep our family home, but me and Wendy were now set for a partnership in life. It was a little emotional from there on in, we headed back to the nick gates together, said our goodbyes, and I headed back to my cell for the night while Wendy headed down to the pub down the road where family and friends were waiting to congratulate her.

That night I drifted off to sleep by myself, as content as I'd ever been in any of these places, dreaming of my

Wendy and the next time I'd see her. Not the traditionally wedding day, but I'll never forget it and it was still perfect to me.

Those dreams were quickly shattered when I was hauled into the Governor's office soon after and shanghaied from Lindholme for strong-arming. I was a lairy bastard selling drugs back then, apparently, and they wanted rid.

One of the screws had approached me "Broughton get your kit, you're going down the block."

I pulled a screw to one side and asked what I was being brought in for. He said the governor will see you on adjudication. So I made my way across the block to see him.

"Do you know why you're here today Broughton?"

I said "I haven't got a fucking clue Guv"

He went "Oh, I think you do... Strong-arming!"

I said "Strong-arming? What the fucks that? Are you having a laugh?"

He went "Bullying"

"Bullying? What do you mean? When have you ever known me to bully anyone?"

He said "You know the score Broughton, we know you're selling".

So I just went "What do you expect me to do?" That wasn't the right response but the logical thinking of any man who was being had over for money.

"Come again?" He said.

"What do you expect me to do, they want their gear but they don't want to pay, how's that bullying?"

He was lost for words, but the outcome was going to be the same regardless, so they sent me off to Hull, to a proper prison again, shanghaied again for strong-arming non-paying drug addicts, what a fucking joke.

HULL AND BACK!

'1990'

'HM Prison Hull is a Category B men's 'local' prison located in Kingston upon Hull in the East Riding of Yorkshire. The term 'local' meaning that the prison, mostly, holds people on remand to the local courts. The prison is still operated by Her Majesty's Prison Service to this day, unlike some of the UK's nicks, which are now privately run cash cows.

Today Hull holds mostly remand, sentenced and convicted males. Prisoners are employed in the workshops, kitchens, gardens and waste management departments. Education classes are also available to prisoners, a far cry from what it was back when I stayed there. Back then it was a real gaol and one which has forged stories about big name cons from all over the country, it certainly wasn't a local prison from what I saw. Every bad man in the UK has spent time in Hull at some point including some serious names from the underworld, the Richardsons, The Lambrianous, Roy Shaw, a few of The Great Train Robbers , Bronson, my good pal Sykesy and few more dangerous types.

At the time of my stay in Hull it was home to some of the most notorious and dangerous faces in the country, though some of them, including my good friend Sykesy, has been moved on to an experimental 'Special Unit' away from the other prisoners.

I'd been given four months for driving whilst banned, a simple misdemeanour but one that cost me dearly. To be straight to the point I missed the birth of my first son Billy, because I was hauled up in the shovel on that pathetic charge.

Back in those days, whether it be an armed blag or a simple driving offence, I didn't abide by the laws of the land. I was already banned from driving for various minor offences but it didn't deter me from still running nice motors and driving around with the rest of the legit. crowd on the public highways. With hindsight it was a massive mistake and certainly not a crime that justified me missing my son's birth.

At the time I had a big white E190 Merc, that I used to cruise about in, me and some of the lads from my firm all had Mercs, real 'drug dealer type' motors, everyone on the estate was putting two and two together and getting five. Yes we were crooked but our crimes were of a much more traditional nature. I won't name those guys from our small firm, but I hope they're having a read and getting the opportunity to reminisce.

Before arriving at Hull I'd been up in front of Stypendery Magistrates. I was in for next to nothing, a crime of the common man. I explained fully the circumstances that Wendy was due very soon, the judge listened intently and my hopes grew. He paused for thought and then looked me straight in the eye and shook his head. I was a regular here and leniency didn't apply, in a strange way that makes sense, but given what I would miss out on I just couldn't accept it. The prick gave me four months, I couldn't believe it. I simply called him an "Old bastard" and fucked off down the stairs, absolutely downtrodden. Crompton was his name, the puppeteer of Stypendry Magistrates, strangely enough he was also the Headmaster at Walthyoff School when I lived on the Manor, perhaps he'd remembered me. He knew me back then and he'd grown to dislike me. I was sure I'd heard you couldn't be tried by a Magistrate that knew you personally, seems in this case not.

The way in which I'd been convicted for those driving offences was laughable to say the least. Me and a pal had gone over to a club in Nottingham by the name of The Black Orchid. I'd driven, knowing I was already banned. We'd headed back to Sheffield for the last hour and the police had clocked us on the way back.

We'd outrun the police, but they'd caught up with us later on outside another club, Sinatra's in town. I was adamant that it was my pal who had been driving and he even had the keys on him to back the story up. There was no way this one would stick.

By the time the court case came around and after a couple of basic questions; my pal came out with the epic line, "No Clyde only drove to Nottingham, he didn't drive back, I 'were' driving."

My barrister turned and looked at the judge in amazement and said "Well, as you can see your honour, this hasn't been rehearsed" The courtroom broke out in hysterics.

I had to take it easy on my pal, he was a straight kid, he wasn't used to having to stand up in court and think on his feet, but his stupidity that day had astounded me.

I didn't spend long in there, but there were a couple of significant events and some of the best stories I'd gleaned from Dave Lee were from Hull, mostly centring around our mutual friend Sykesy and his run-ins with notorious faces from the other side of the country, which included Bronson, Roy Shaw and the Richardsons.

Hull had a 'Special Unit' on 'A' Wing. They were conducting an experiment behind locked doors, testing a softly, softly regime on some of the most dangerous and disruptive inmates sent from long term dispersal jails, which sounds like utter madness I know. The special unit was volatile from the start, with a guy named David McAllister who was serving nineteen years for armed robbery and assault even managing to escape. The prisoners arrived from punishment blocks all over the country, ones who'd been in constant trouble, it was an attempt to break that cycle. This came at a time when prison resources were already stretched, the unit cost nearly a million pounds and was very heavily staffed.

Prior to entering the Special Unit my pal Sykesy had been on segregation, he was serving two and half years for burglary and assault, and three and a half years on top for assaulting staff whilst in Hull. On the day he went down the block a restraint team with helmets and shields were drafted in, but they managed to talk him down their quietly. There was little chance I would see him during my time in Hull while ever he was cooped in that Special Unit.

Like I said I was in the shovel when our Billy, my oldest son, was born. I was working the Kitchens in Hull nick, when I found out Wendy had gone into labour. At t

I'd been informed in the morning that Wend y had gone into labour. At the time I was padded up with Eddie Wharton, the brother of boxer Henry. I'd finished my duties in the kitchen for the day and headed back to my cell, riddled with worry / anxiety. I was het up with tension wondering how Wendy was getting on, had my boy arrived on planet earth yet, were they both OK.

The lads on my landing had assured me everything would be alright. Me, Ronnie Barton, Albert Barton, Eddie Wharton, Flap aka Wolf, were sat around tentatively waiting for some news.

One of the lads suggested we have a smoke to lighten the mood, there was nothing I could do stuck in that cell. We rolled a joint and passed it around the cell to take the edge off. My anxiety must have rubbed off onto my cell mates, they appeared as much in need of it as I did.

"Broughton! Your Wife's just given birth to a baby boy" A yell came through the cell bars, like the announcement of the arrival of the day's newspaper.

Just at that same moment a cloud of pungent weed smoke, Hull's finest, wafted through the bars and hit him like a truck. He knew now wasn't the time or place to take issue with the consumption of a low level substance like that and trotted merrily on his way.

"Congratulations... by the way" The screw added as he fucked off down the landing almost choking on the fumes.

The lads gave me the obligatory pat on the back, we finished our joint and meandered off to sleep. I drifted off totally content, knowing my boy was waiting for me on the other side and that my beloved Wendy was doing fine.

Billy was born in 1990 and Danny was born later in 1994. I think I'd stated that I'd always lived life without regret, but maybe there was the odd occasion. With hindsight getting banged up when my Wendy only had three weeks to go with our Billy was a massive mistake, but from their things blossomed, I was still a wrong un, but Wendy kept me on track and our family began to grow with the birth of my sons.

SHANGHAIED

'A Dozen Eggs'

After the glassing incident I did a quick 6 months in the Victorian stronghold that is Armley, Leeds. The days passed steadily, I spent my time mostly working as a cleaner in the association areas, gyms and occasionally the kitchens. I quickly went back to being a gym orderly, the role I was accustomed to in most nicks, right up my street, and never a punishment in my eyes.

Whilst there I spent a brief nine weeks working in the kitchens, I say brief as a small, not significant, but comical incident in there ended up getting me deported to another prison much further afield.

I was working alongside a good pal of mine, a Mackem from Sunderland, Tommy Mason, a great kid who I'd met in the nick. Tommy was a habitual offender much like myself, a jovial guy who'd get into trouble for fun or to satisfy his gluttonous appetite. Some people just pass you by in those places and some remain your friends forever, Tommy was one of those long time friends only gaol can produce. He always had my back and always kept me well fed.

I was in the kitchen on one particular day and the kitchen lads were all getting their breakfast when one of the kids who worked in the their took six eggs and put them on his tray, now that was greed, pure greed, we weren't starved in there in the least, especially as kitchen hands, if anything we were positively spoilt. I looked down at the tray of about fifty eggs, and I thought fuck it I'll do the same, bomf, bomf, bomf ... six eggs went on to my tray and off I went, if it was good for the goose it was good for the gander. But before I'd even got back to my table the resident screw, by the name of Campbell, shouted over "Broughton what do you think you are doing?"

I went "I'm having the same as him." Knowing that wouldn't wash.

He went "He's cooked em, you can't have six?" Talking shite as ever.

"Are you fuckin shagging him?" His defence of the guy and his beloved eggs was making no sense, I should have kept my mouth shut though, a comment like that wasn't going to bode well with the board if I got pulled in.

"Anyway, ye can bollocks, I'm having em." And quickly fucked off back to my cell.

I got back to my pad and started eating them as quick as I could, not quite in the vein of Paul Newman in the famous prison film Cool Hand Luke, even getting six eggs down sharpish is still a task when the screws are on your back and your fellow inmates are rolling about laughing at you trying to get them down. Scoffing away, with the realisation a few hours later I'd be egg-bound, or constipated, however you want to put it.

The next minute the Burglars (Screws / PO's) have come charging in to the dining area looking for me, yelling "Get back to your cells." It was the overreaction of the century, it seemed I'd caused some serious problems for myself.... again.

Two minutes later, my mate Tommy wanders into my cell and I said "What's up?"

He replied "Fuck it, if they're sacking you, then they're sacking me n'all". Tommy was number one in the kitchen at that time he sorted everything out, knew it inside out, a real good worker, but he had principles.

Within a couple of hours I'd been re-allocated to Acklington in Northumberland. Now I know I've been about a bit in the prison system, but if you look at the reasons, sometimes justified, sometimes not, but wasting taxpayers' money on a move like that just didn't stack up.

Me and my mate Tommy from Sunderland were well and truly separated, while I'm sure he would have been happy to go way up north to the likes of Acklington, instead they sent Tommy to Ranby which is over in Retford, Nottingham way. They were forever playing games, making our visits difficult, dividing friendships.

I was left to ponder, did I really need to eat those six eggs?

*   *   *   *

Acklington was full to the brim at the time and I'd had to wait until there was a space for me, and the obvious stepping stone between there and Leeds was HM Prison Durham. A Category 'B' men's prison, located in the Elvet area of Durham which held just over a thousand inmates.

I was only there for a few weeks, but while I was in Durham nick, I was on association and this bunch of kids I'd palled up with when a lad came running down the landing, screaming and carrying on. I had no reason to run, so I stood and waited to see what all the commotion was about.

"Fucking hell, what is it?' I expected to see Godzilla come storming through the gaol any minute.

"He's just been brought in" Who the fuck were they on about.

And who walked through Sykes! Every last one of them was hiding out of the way and there were some right hard core prisoners in that jail at the time. There was a kid called Harry Perry from Carlisle and a guy from Newcastle called Steve 'Snowy' Abingdon. Even they just stood up, went upstairs and got behind their doors. I'm not saying they were scared, more likely just didn't want any hassle.

"Sykesy" I shouted.

"Clyde!" He replied in a warm welcoming tone.

That would help the week pass I thought, if only I could have stayed a little longer. We had a couple of games of chess and went down the gym, as we always did, but a week or so later we had to say our goodbyes when I was moved on. If Durham knew what was good for them they'd have kept me on board, I was one of the few in the system, along with Delroy, who could tame the beast, keep him occupied enough to get him out of the screws hair and save a few jaws being broken in the process. All he needed was a distraction, but the authorities hadn't really cottoned on yet.

Before I knew it I was on my way to Acklington in Northumberland, twelve miles from the Scottish border, it felt almost foreign, the change in climate was noticeable and the thick Scottish accent of the screws and the local cons made that stay hard work.

I'd spent a steady three hours getting thrown around in the back of the meat wagon to arrive at that fucking dump.

It wasn't long before I was shanghaied again for an even more bizarre reason. I only spent about three weeks in Acklington and my little foreign holiday was over, a veritable one star all inclusive, but it was three weeks too long in my eyes. By some unbelievable coincidence I'd been confused with another inmate also by the name of Clyde Broughton, and was duly shifted out. The crazy thing was by the time that little matter of confusion was resolved, I'd already been moved on, and as it turned out the 'other' Clyde was actually a black guy from Scotland, how fucking wrong could these people be.

Anyway I breathed a sigh of relief when I got moved on back to Lindholme in my native South Yorkshire ready for dispersal. Much nearer home and ideal for release.

As my sentence neared its conclusion the days passed by a little more quickly. I knew I needed to keep out of trouble for the sake of my loved ones. If I got into trouble and was moved further afield and they had to trek to the other side of the country to come see me then I knew the visits would be few and far between.

SLEEPER

'The Indian Game Bird'

My last sentence had passed quick, I'd done a good wedge of it on remand and it seemed to fly by. I'd had enough of the nick, for now, and needed something to occupy my time and keep me out of trouble. I'd always had a knack for the outdoor pursuits, whether it be; hawking, hare coursing, even dog fighting, you name it. Make of it what you will, and I'm not boasting at all, but in the animal race, bloodshed s part of nature, the small interference of man is hardly something new. I've kept animals all my life and can honestly say I've loved them all, but to deny them the opportunity to do what comes naturally is equally as cruel as some of the activities you may disagree with. It's a tricky one, there is a balance and I believe I had it somewhere about right, you may think different, but regardless those days are long behind me and seem like a different era altogether.

For a spell I became involved in the world of Cock Fighting. It started off as a bit of fun with some friends but as with everything I was involved with, it wasn't long before I was playing for bigger stakes. I'd initially gotten into cock fighting through my cousin 'our Kevin', he had a load of 'Bantis' as we'd call them. Him and a guy who lived on City Road by the name of Alan Bales used to breed them. I'd only tagged along to a fight one day for something to do and the rest was history, my interest in the sport, if you could call it that, was cemented.

We used to meet on the Pigeon Coytes every Sunday afternoon to fight Cockerills. Only little Banti-cotes, but they were really game. They'd fight to the death, they wouldn't go for it and eventually quit, there was generally only one outcome, and it was usually final. Those things weren't wired up right, even when they're losing they act they're winning and keep going, not like you or I, who might know when to quit. They'd have been fighting whether a tenner was being waved under their beak or not.

They might have two or three fights a day some of those birds. Only small friendly stakes were exchanged, say a tenner or twenty quid at a push, but never much more than that, unless someone had 'had a few' and got carried away, but that was rare.

I'd gotten right into, a bit more so than the other lads, even the ones who'd introduced me to it and it wasn't long before my birds were fighting for bigger stakes and I was arranging to meet-up with people outside of that small circle for our animals to fight.

I was immersed in the whole idea, I did a lot of research and even read a few books down the library on the subject before I went and bought myself an Indian Game Bird, a baby, not something you would find generally on a farm over here in the UK. Those types of birds are bred specifically for fighting over in India and little else. It cost me about a hundred and fifty quid, which was a song back then.

I'd bought the bird from an Asian guy over in Maltby. They look what they are, bred for 'feytin'. Back in 1849, long before cock-fighting was outlawed in this country. Heavy and muscular with a large breast and wide set leg, they have tight feathering and no fluff, all qualities ideal for the fight game. I called him Sleeper because he used to put the competition to sleep pretty much every time.

So anyway I brought my new prospect back from Maltby, and right away set about getting him fit in it's Avery, more like a pen. I used to hang a cabbage from the mesh roofing, so if the bird wanted to eat it had to jump up, forcing it to use the muscles in its legs, a key part of their armoury, when they're 'feyting' that's what they use, they kick and they peck. Jumping was the best possible thing they could do to build strength. It wasn't like I could teach it to do press-ups, ultimately its own greed helped condition it. They've got to have the physique to last the fight, the longer they last the more of a chance they have of winning, or indeed surviving. It's the same in cock fighting as dog fighting you can't train these animals to fight but you make them fit for the fight.

I had another mate who never trained his but thought he was the man in the cock fighting game. He just used to let his birds roam freely in their pen all week and then make them fight come Sunday afternoon.

I went down one day with my Indian Game bird, no money involved, and he had a Golden Duck Wing. They set about it and mine had it down on the floor, pulled its fucking tongue out, its eye out, the lot. What he didn't realise was he was fighting against a bird that was bred to fight, not something you'd find on the average farm. Farmers do have Duck Wings, and they can fight, but nothing in comparison to what I had. Like a Staffy against a Pitbull, one a pet the other a born killing machine.

I'd put the word out that I had this 'reyt good bird', and some gypsies came over to see me from a big camp over in Tinsley. A massive gyppo camp, absolutely huge, it's big, cock fighting, in their circles and they don't like playing for peanuts, it's a bravado thing, if you put the most money up you've already won, because everyone thinks you're the big man. The Prices, the Collins, the Mullins's, were all on that same site and all names you knew to avoid if you had any sense.

I know abroad and possibly some people over here use spurs (daggers attached to their claws), but we didn't it was just two cocks going at it in the open, not even penned in. We just loved to watch the free fight and the gameness of the birds, the animals natural inclination to attack / kill. I should imagine when they've got blades on their legs there's a possibility that a bad bird can beat a good one, it only takes one trip or slip, or a lucky shot, but ours was a real, fair, competition.

So we headed down to the Gypsy Camp, just me and a couple of pals, Dave Ager and Alan Bailes. There were hundreds waiting there, I kid you not it, it was a massive site, I reckon there were nearly a hundred and fifty trailers on that site.

The stakes had already been set, three hundred pound, winner takes all. Decent money then, and even now, and much higher than the ten or twenty pound stakes me and my friends were used to.

So anyway the fight started and my bird 'Sleeper' is off to a flyer, he's booting this other bird all over the shop. He was getting the better of the opponent and it kept turning around, then shooting off. Sleeper was chasing it down, he wanted the kill. The other bird running away, no different to a Boxer turning his back in the ring, Sykes and Gardner sprang to mind, reason enough to call the fight off there and then.

I was pretty green (naïve) to the rules of the sport. I'd jumped straight in at the deep end as usual and assumed this was a fight to death, like we did up the Pigeon Coyts on a Sunday Afternoon. Just because it was running away it didn't mean I'd won. Instead of just standing his ground and crowing, beating his chest like King Kong it was chasing the cunt all over the camp, burning up even more precious energy.

The two birds ended up under a Lorry, still battling away, they weren't penned in. As they came out, a fucking Jack Russell ran up and joined in the commotion. It could have gone for either bird but it ran up to mine and bit it on the wing. I could see it had shaken him and he was no longer as game as he had been from the off.

Then came the icing on the game, a little gyppo kid came along and booted my bird right up the arse, it left the fucking floor. What the fuck was going on, it seemed like I was being done out of £300 quid, these gyppos weren't taking any chances and put some little kid on the payroll. They knew my bird was overpowering there's from the off and they were protecting their investment.

That was that, after being bitten by a Jack Russell and booted up the arse by a little pikey kid my bird quit, it'd had enough, it was tough, but it couldn't fight cocks, dogs and gyppos all at the same time.

I was gutted. Vastly outnumbered, green to the rules of the sport and mightily pissed off I reluctantly paid the man (Caesar Price) and said "Keep my fuckin bird n'all, its wank." I left the camp totally deflated with no intentions of ever buying another bird or carrying on with the sport.

Later than night I was back down the Springwood drowning my sorrows and having a pint with my old pal Wally Cooper. Were chatting away and he asked me what I'd been up to. I said I've been cock fighting and reeled off my sorrowful tale of how my prize bird had lost. Wally knew everything about those types of sports (and any other subject you could care to mention) and immediately wanted to know more about how it had actually gone down.

Now this guy I'm sat with is in to everything, intrigue crossed his face, his tone picked up "Hold up, tell me again exactly what happened." His intrigue appearing to grow.

So I told him "It started off reyt, my bird giving it some fuckin hammer, but the other bird kept turning and running off." Still under the impression I'd lost.

"Running off?" He said.

"Yeah running off. My bird 'were' having to chase it," I told him again.

He went "Let me tell you summat Clyde in cock feytin, soon as a bird turns its back it's like a boxing match, they're done, it's over," Who'd have thought the rules would be so regimented.

I said "So what happens if one of their dogs bit it and a little gyppo kid kicked it up the arse? How's that sit within the rule book?" He nearly spat out his fucking pint.

He laughed "Fuckin hell Clyde you've been robbed, straight up!" What the fuck!

It was now eleven o'clock at night, I'd had two or three pints and my perspective was starting to adjust.

Clyde "Tha won," He carried on.

I said "You fuckin what? Have you got' car outside?" I already knew he did, he didn't need to reply.

We headed for the door and jumped straight in, this man knew the rules and would be there to back me up morally if things didn't get sorted, but my temper was up and the rules weren't so important now anyway. We drove back down to the gyppo site, it was eleven at night, the place was huge, lights dotted all around, it looked like a little city of its own as we drove down the makeshift track to the main man's trailer.

I marched straight up to his caravan. Caesar Price, a big name in the gypsy community, or at least round our way. I banged on his door, it felt like it was made out of cardboard, I'm surprised my fist hadn't gone straight through it, I was now nearing boiling point.

Boom! Boom! Boom! "Caesar! Fucking ger out here!" I bellowed.

Lights were starting to come on all over the camp, doors opening, gorillas trampling over, kids, dogs the lot, vests were coming off anything that thought it could fight and that wasn't just the blokes.

The fat slob opened the door half asleep "What's up?"

I said "You fuckin know what's up, you lost that fight my bird got kicked, bit, your bird fuckin ran off! I want my fuckin money back!".

His face the epitome of guilt. I carried on "I want my money back and I want my fuckin bird back n' all."

He knew he was out of order and he knew I meant business and didn't want the hassle, he said "You're bird is round the back" Reluctantly.

I was starting to think a little straighter now, massively outnumbered, a head full of steam or not, what the fuck was I doing wondering round the back of a gyppo's caravan at eleven at night, I must be fucking stupid.

By this time things had gone too far, I had to see it through, I'd had a few pints and that'd made me grow six inch. I went round the back and the bird was in one of those big old horse transporter boxes. I grabbed the bird off its perch and stuck it under my arm like the morning paper, it didn't so much as flinch, it knew it's master was back and was probably still shattered form the fight. He gave me the money without much hassle, for a pikey, he knew it wasn't his anyway.

As I'm walking out I noticed he's got this English Bull Terrier chained up by the side of this trailer, so I unlinked it and dragged it off with me and shouted back "I'm tekkin this bastard n' all." His jaw still on the floor.

Price was stood there speechless. It was a small price to pay for his bad sportsmanship. I slung them both in the car and we made our exit. As it turned out the dog was actually deaf, and actually a bitch, but she made a lovely pet and I kept her for some time.

Roy Jones the ex-professional boxer also liked to partake in a few blood sports, cocks fighting / Pitbulls etc. I met him once, in fact there's a signed picture of him hanging in my bar of him with my son Billy. He charged me twenty quid for the privilege, it seems everyone was on the take it that game, not just Caesar.

LIFE ON THE TICK

'Mercedes E190'

My life continued to meander along in no particular direction. I wasn't out blagging jewellery shops or mugging folk anymore, those days were over, but the undertone of criminality still followed me wherever I went. I'd learnt from those early incidents in my early criminal career and had vowed not to take those kinds of risks again, in whatever field I would apply myself.

Financially though, things were ticking over nicely and I'd had a pretty good run without any problems from the law. To confirm it I had a three year old Mercedes parked outside the house, full body-kit the lot, a proper 'drug dealer's' motor as some would put it. It certainly stood out on our estate, though I have to admit it was appropriated on the back of some very dubious financial arrangements, I could never have afforded it in reality.

The finance had been brokered by a guy I'd met through a friend of a friend. A real clever bloke from over in Barnsley by the name of Tony Wall. He was, for want of a better term, a 'master fraudster'. He'd spent most of his life scamming banks and other financial institutions through the use of counterfeit paperwork. It was all he knew and he was always more than happy to hook someone else up with the relevant paperwork for a commission. Why wouldn't he? He was still getting the rewards but taking a lot less risk, unless someone grassed him up of course, but that was rare in our circles and even if they did all he had to do was deny it. Tony knew everything, and I mean everything, about scams and deception, he couldn't sleep at night if he hadn't told at least three decent lies that day.

After some short negotiations on how the arrangement would work, and more importantly to him how much I'd have to kick back, we were in his car and heading over to Speeds, a car dealership in Chesterfield, a slightly more upmarket area with the right clientele to warrant a Merc garage and just far enough out of town for me not to raise suspicions as a known face. In truth I had no choice but to go out of town, a Merc garage would never have flown in our area.

I walked into the dealership with clear intent on what I'd come to purchase, everything else was simply a formality. They, the sales team, lapped it up, in other circumstances I'd have been sweating like a pig, hoping not to be rumbled, but I knew Tony was an expert in his field and there wasn't even a hint of suspicion, or doubt of my credibility, on their part.

For the next half an hour I felt like I really was the Mayor of Chesterfield, they couldn't do enough for me. The papers were signed and the deed was done. I'd passed with flying colours, a few formalities were carried out and I would be back to pick up the car in just a few days. Pretty soon I would be the proud owner of a 'D' reg Mercedes E190, worth about £15K (£21K with the finance of nearly £460 per month). I'd had to put my 3.0 litre Senator down towards the Merc, and a £2,200 deposit, but that was nothing in the scheme of things.

Tony had also told me to take out an insurance policy, which was another £15 per month, so that in the event I lost my job, the one I'd provided wage slips for, cheers Tony, they'd cover the car payments until I was back on my feet.

The scams with Tony never stopped, I became as addicted to them as he was. In 1989 I ended up getting a house in my name over in Barnsley and a ten thousand pound cash loan from Lloyds bank to build dog kennels, as I was a breeder obviously, that was kind of a half truth, I did keep dogs.

The Finance companies were taking a real a real kick in the bollocks at the hands of my pal Tony, and his arrangements really suited me. In return for brokering the deal on the house I got to keep the £10K from the loan and was paid £600 per month for having my name against the house until it was switched over and ultimately became his.

Things didn't stop there. He's told me there was a new breed of scammer coming through, one who exploited the blasé nature in which the insurance companies were paying out for people being injured on the high street. The authorities had deep pockets, didn't want the bad publicity and ultimately found it very hard to disprove someone's discomfort.

A policy was put in place that covered loss of earnings, again this would have to be backed up with fake wage slips at some point. In order to cash in on the insurance I had to stage an accident and it needed to be in front of an independent witness, so I was on the lookout for one of the more gullible ones. We could have used our own decoy, but what was the point, there was a risk of association and you had to pay the fucker.

I had 'my little accident' on a dreary day in Barnsley, a badly concealed sunken kerb, I'd tripped over it, conveniently near a phone box. I'd made sure that a passing 'old dear' had seen me fall. I pretended to be completely knocked out, while she rang an ambulance, and then spent half a day playing silly bastards down the hospital.

I was off work with immediate effect. Everything was getting paid for and I was getting £600 per month for being on the sick as an out of work landscape gardener.

Even the insurance premiums were free for the first three months on that policy and that was when the accident happened, by no coincidence.

These types of arrangements continued for three years, until eventually I got pulled in. They couldn't prove anything, they pulled Tony as well. In some respects it was legit, the paperwork supported it, it was fraud, not straight theft and our clerical adversaries could prove no different. I was in for eight hours, I kept my gob shut and it went no further, but the Old Bill had a result in one way, because I'd be calling it a day with those types of scam from then on.

That little scare made me re-evaluate the things I was doing with Tony, yes he knew what he was doing and yes they couldn't prove anything, but with my history I knew there would forever be someone on my case trying to make head nor tail of how I'd obtained things, so I decided to end my arrangements with Tony and we went our separate ways.

Tony lived at Staincross in a big bungalow, he was a really clued up guy, but he started going daft in the end or so it appeared. We'd walk into a pub, just me and him, and he'd order twelve pints of lager all at once, and only drink one, whether he was doing it as part of another scam I have no idea. Maybe it was his backup plan for getting pulled, grounds of insanity, I never worked it out.

* * * *

Calling it a day with the deceptions couldn't have come at a better time. It was around this time that my second son, Danny, was born in 1994, to be precise, and luckily for me this time I wasn't banged up and could attend the birth.

I wasn't about to miss the birth of my boy this time around for anything. I still needed to graft, but my activities were VERY low key in the run up to his birth. For a short spell I was reluctant to even go out, or associate with my criminal friends. If I happened to be in the wrong place at the wrong time, or even offered a decent opportunity to earn I knew I wouldn't be able to turn it down, so it was better not be around those types of people or places at all. I couldn't afford to miss out on the birth of my second son, as well as our Billy, it would kill me and if it didn't then Wendy would.

I'd vowed to keep myself out of prison for the kid's sake, but crime was all I knew. Sure I had the faculties to lug things around and carry out the requirements of a real job, but it just wasn't me. I couldn't answer to others, I had to do things for myself, but there was one more sentence to be served before I could finally put crime behind me.

SHOPLIFTING

'Eighteen Months!?, 1998'

What's the longest you've heard anyone get for Shoplifting? A couple of weeks, a few months maybe. How about eighteen months? No way, that couldn't happen you're saying, not even to a repeat offender. Well it did and it happened to me.

The very last time I was in prison was in 1998. I went to Leeds first, for a very short spell and then onto Ranby. I'd been using counterfeit credit cards all across Yorkshire and eventually been caught, but the charge was 'shoplifting' which normally I'd have been happy with. Though I'm no computer wizard if there was a crime or a scam going down I was usually roped in. I got pulled in Birstall, over Batley way. Here's how it came about.

My mate Billy Barnes, who I'd first met in Walton nick, and a well known criminal who'd done a few big sentences himself, got in touch with a little proposition. Billy was from Leeds, and had been in and out of the system all his life The first time I'd met him he was doing eleven years for robbery and the second time I'd met him was on the outside and he told me he'd done another ten for bringing brown back from Holland, he'd been caught on Hull docks and that was after being out for only six weeks, absolute madness.

He'd recently gotten out again and I bumped into him in the Travellers Pub on City Road in Sheffield, he was sat drinking with another well known villain from our neck of the woods, an old school villain by the name of Dougie Parkes.

So I'm just stood there with my pals, having a few pints and a few laughs, when I heard this voice say "Mr Broughton" I turned around and there was Billy Barnes. That was it, old friendships never take long to reignite, where you living, what you up to, you know how it goes.

So we'd been drinking all night and he told me he had a flat on Norfolk Park in Sheffield. I went to see him the next day to talk business, he asked me what I was into, trying to get the measure of whether I'd be interested in running one of his scams, before bringing me onboard.

He said, if I wanted it, he had some work for me and a friend, counterfeit credit cards. They worked but they didn't go through the swipe system and needed manually processing, all we had to do was gather a little information on local addresses and we were good to go. I didn't know how the in's and out's of the scam worked, nor did I need to know, but we were guaranteed a £2,000 transaction would go through on every card, and it never failed, not even once. The only thing we had to do was go into a different town, nip into the local post office and ask for the postcode of the adjacent street, and then get the number of a house on that street, remember you couldn't just look it up on the internet back in those days.

Every time we went to make a purchase, the swipe would initially fail, then they'd have to manually input some information which is where the address and postcode came in and Bob's your uncle, it would go straight through. The name and address weren't cross referenced, the shop assistant was blind to the con, if the system said it was OK, it was OK, even if they had their suspicions they had no real means of backing up their suspicions, we never encountered any problems.

Eventually we were buying to order, never struggling to turn our goods back into cash, most wanted the latest big Toshiba Televisions, they were £1500 quid at the time and we were doing them half price. Video recorders, computers etc. we were backed up with orders. Initially Billy had told us what to go and buy, but as word spread in our circles we had our own orders to fulfil, all we had to do was kick back the agreed percentage to Billy and we could do as we pleased. We were making good money out of it, sometimes a few hundred quid a day and this went on for months, three cards a week, different towns, we did a lot of travelling, mostly electrical shops.

One day we'd gone in to Batley (Birstall), the transaction had gone through, no problems, as usual. Then on our way home we thought sod it and nipped into Wakefield to get another one of the items from our list, our downfall being it was the exact same item we'd just purchased in Batley. It wasn't in stock and before we knew it they'd rung through and asked the Batley store if it was available. The person at the other end of the phone said "Funnily we've just sold one of those to a couple of guys," It didn't take long for them to smell a rat and they rang the police. They were not quite sure what we were up to, but they knew something wasn't right. By the time the police arrived we were bang to rights and found in possession of various bits and pieces associated with credit card fraud that cemented the old bill's suspicions of how we were operating.

When it came to court the laws hadn't quite adapted themselves to deal with that type of crime, it was relatively new, unlike now. So in the absence of any suitable legislation we were prosecuted for SHOPLIFTING! Can you believe it? Possibly the lamest crime on my rap sheet.

The mate of mine who'd travelled everywhere with me was a bit of a drifter, not a tramp or a vagrant, but a man who never felt any particular ties to anywhere, unlike me and my beloved Sheffield.

He said "Clyde, fuck this, I'm doing one, feel free to point the finger at me, they're not gonna find me," Giving me his blessing to put him in the frame and make my life easier.

In normal circumstances I'd never have done that, but it was agreed between the two of us. I was never a drifter myself, I liked the home life, if I wasn't in the nick I was in Sheffield, nowhere else, but if I was, I'd like to think, I'd have done the same for him, though possibly not, I'm a bit of a ruthless cunt when it comes down to it.

I ended up getting eighteen months, 18 months for Shoplifting! That might have been some kind of justice system record at the time. I was headed straight to Leeds and then on to Ranby to finish my sentence.

Billy Barnes never got brought into it. He didn't need to. He'd told me he was leaving for Africa and I haven't seen or heard from him since, though I'd love to hear from him if this tale makes it that far.

* * * *

After a very brief stay in Leeds pending allocation, I was on my way to Ranby for shoplifting. Me, Clyde Broughton banged up for shoplifting. If Dave Lee, Sykesy, or any of my other criminal peers, were still alive they would have positively pissed themselves at the idea.

As ever my stay there came with a few somewhat incidental, but humorous incidents. One being the fact that our lass had been sending my letters to Rampton! Not Ranby, what did she think I was? I was in for Shoplifting, I wasn't a Serial Killer.

I was out in the yard one day when who did I clap eyes on? None other than Dehavilland, the guy whose depositions I'd read whilst in Wakefield. He was playing Volleyball out in the yard like butter wouldn't melt. I asked around just to double check, the other prisoners knew him as something else, but I knew who he really was. I played it down, said I must have been mistaken, I wasn't scared of the guy, but I didn't want to be involved in any bullshit, I just wanted to be on my way home. Whilst in Ranby, he ended up having a relationship with his Psychiatrist from the outside, then he got moved on because he'd told a female prison screw that he'd love to fuck her. You just couldn't get away with that, especially a man with his background.

Whilst I was in Ranby my father passed away. I regret being in there at such a critical time, but I hadn't seen it coming.

The nurse had rung the nick during the day to say he was critical. I asked the screws if I could go see him, it wasn't a definite no, but none of them were willing to take me. Later that night I got the call to say he'd passed away. They let me out for the funeral, even removed the cuffs temporarily, but that day was an emotional one and I was grateful they'd let me attend. God bless my Father.

DRIFTING

'Crack...'

Just like any job or trade, criminality was no different, it's still work and it can still get tedious, don't get me wrong it was a lot more exciting than your average nine while five, but if you haven't had a good score for a spell you can grow despondent with the game just like anything else.

I'd been drifting for a while, I was making good money week in, week out from a bit of this and that, but it wasn't exciting me like it used to. The jewellery thefts, the burglaries, the getaway cars, those things were all long gone, and things were becoming a little tedious and I will admit for a spell I lost my way, just a little. I'd lost heart with the game so to speak. I was comfortable financially, but the buzz wasn't quite enough. The good old days of smash and grab were long gone. Advancements in forensics, CCTV were becoming more common place, the options were less, the odds forever tipping in the law's favour.

Various things happened over those couple of years that I'd become discontent, some I'd prefer to brush over, but I was always active, always up to something, but it wasn't the same any more, perhaps I needed to get pulled, do a short stint back inside to wake me up again, make me hungry for release.

Over what felt like years, but in reality was only about eighteen months my involvement with certain characters from the area and my dealings associated with them, often put me in the wrong circles at times, and for a spell I'd taken to smoking crack. It was offered and I hadn't refused, it wasn't a cry for help, more a kick back at boredom, the monotony of life on the estate. I can honestly say the hit from crack was better than anything else I'd ever sampled, straight up, and I can see why people get drawn in.

I was still grafting plenty but I was at it every single day, not through the pipe but in a spliff, so it wasn't as intense but it had definitely taken a hold on me for a short spell and it needed sorting. That period lasted for a good fourteen or fifteen months.

I never had a problem in that I hadn't stooped so low it was my sole purpose, but I definitely let it get a little out of hand. I never sold anything to pay for it, because I was always earning, but it was a genuine problem and for a spell I was smoking it every single day.

Luckily I had a moment of clarity, I was on a mate's bike and had just picked up some crack. I was smoking it, and something just clicked in my head, I was never going to get a bigger buzz than the first one, the first buzz was always the best. I dropped it there and then. I rattled for a few days and normality was resumed, I'd emerged from the other side of that dark period a stronger character.

About two years later I was in the exact same spot, on the same kids bike, when I stumbled on the crack dealer, so I said "Giz a bit?"

He handed it over, I'd been completely clean now for some time. But that put my mind to rest, it was that good, but not the same, I knew I should never touch it again, and I didn't continue, I was testing myself and I'd passed the test with flying colours.

I've seen the inside of a few junkies houses and they have nothing, they sell everything off, rip everyone off, I never got anywhere close to that but I can see how addiction to that stuff can spiral out of control.

Now I at no point considered myself a junkie, but I guess I never would have, but I'm sure a few people can relate to that meandering, sinking way of life.

Everyone has their vices, and lord knows I like a drink and the occasional bit of 'this and that' but you've always got to retain an element of control, just like the robberies, burglaries etc. things had to be quantified, risks weighed up. I loved the buzz of a good blag, but if I'd jumped at every opportunity that had come my way I'd have ended up doing a lot more bird than I did, trust me.

Anyway it happened and I have nothing to hide, it never took my soul, but I dare say it could have if I hadn't been so busy grafting.

Around the same time I was interviewed for a regular documentary show that aired on Yorkshire Television by the name of First Tuesday, the same show that had aired the infamous 'Paul Sykes at Large' documentary. It was all about life on the estates of Sheffield and in particular the Manor. The film crew came into my kitchen and I was absolutely steaming drunk. I must have ranted on for nearly an hour, probably making littler sense at all. When it aired a few months later they'd cut my excerpt down to about thirty seconds, I clearly hadn't given them what they wanted, or was so incoherent it wasn't broadcast'able.

Around this time, though I'd fallen into the trap of wasting some of my time smoking crack my good pal Paul Sykes had fallen much deeper into the hole. He was boozing, day and night. He liked to drink, I mean he really liked to drink and he wouldn't recover from that spiral the way I did.

When he came over to Sheffield I'd get meet him off the train. The last time I remember that happening the first thing he did was walk into WH Smith's, got a copy of FHM magazine out and opened it up to a big article on him, 'Britain's Hardest Man' it was titled.

"Look at that Clyde. Hardest man in Britain" He rolled it up and put it in his jacket, with no intention of paying whatsoever. Being pissed up with a title like that to live up to you were never going to last long.

Bang across the road from Sheffield train station, there's a pub called the Howard Hotel. We went straight in there, had a drink and he started rolling a joint in full view of all, he just didn't care, you could imagine what the rest of the day was like. Keeping the wildest dog in the city on a fucking leash was an unenviable task.

We'd venture on and continue to booze in pubs like the Windsor, The Elm Tree and then on to the Springwood, because he wanted to come and meet my mates at the local pub.

I said, "Listen, there's a bloke..." And wondered whether to bother continuing. "Who's a bit of a show-off and he likes to have a fight."

"Somebody my age that likes to have a fight?" Come on Clyde, show me the way!" But luck was on our side that day, he wasn't there and the trouble never materialised.

Towards the end Paul's lifestyle was so disjointed he'd ended up sleeping rough, the stories I'd heard coming back broke my heart. I ventured over to Wakefield a couple of times but never managed to track him down. Hoping to throw him a tenner, go for a pint, get him fed, whatever was needed.

I once went over to see Paul I had no idea him and Cath had split up. I knocked on the door to be met by Cath. She went, "Hello?"

I went, "It's me, Clyde, from Sheffield."

She went, "I know who it is, come on in love,"

I walked in and at the same time this bloke walked straight out.

I went, "Who's that?"

She went, "Oh, me and Paul split up a bit ago, that's my new boyfriend."

She told me where Paul was living. He lived in this flat and when I got there, fucking hell, you could tell he had deteriorated beyond any coming back. The last time I saw

Paul, he was living in that flat, I couldn't even bring myself to stay, he was not the man I knew.

A month or so later my conscience got the better of me. I went back to Wakefield to try and see him again. But I couldn't find him. I asked his sister where he'd be and she told me to try the Ridings shopping centre, so I went down there. I asked security guards there if they'd seen him and they told me he might be down the bus station. I went down there, but by this time it was becoming clear he was living rough and maybe didn't even want to be found. I wanted to find him and give him a bit of help, even though he'd have most probably spent it on booze and whatever else he was getting into. I would have given him a few quid, but I couldn't find him, and nobody could tell me whereabouts he was.

I never found out where / when his funeral was. I wanted to go, but again it never materialised. His whole situation reiterated to me what a close escape I'd had from my little crack episode and gave me further cause to avoid it like the fucking plague.

THE HUSTLE

'Smoking with the Hawk'

I was in need of a few quid, sat in my living room contemplating what I was about to put together. I'd picked up the 'John Paris' cue I'd just bought. It was worth £650, I'd bought it at a competition, cos the bloke 'were' skint, I'd stolen it for just £150 quid. Ronnie O' Sullivan uses the same cue and now so did Clyde Broughton, well in a fashion.

Professional Snooker player and a long time friend of mine Terry Hunt had come over to my house to talk business. I explained to him a little idea I had, a prize match against a guy from Chesterfield.

"He's a good player, you might have heard of him Bob Snell? He's past it now. He's just tried to get on the main tour and failed" The fine details didn't matter to Terry, he was somewhat of an arrogant bastard.

"No problem I'll take his money" He replied. No cracks showing in his confidence.

Now I had every faith in Terry's snooker ability or that he would beat Snell, but being complacent through sheer arrogance was never a good trait, and like it or not, I would be on his back making sure he put the hours in and stayed off the drink in the run up to the match.

A day or so later, I went to meet his opponent Snell and his backer Des at the The Badger Pub on Brockwell Lane in neighbouring Chesterfield, not one of my regulars, but Bob's neck of the woods. Make him feel safe, lure him in, he would never say no on his own manor.

I walked into the pub and spotted Snell and his backer, a big black guy named Des. He looked the business a big burly lad, for want of a better term a 'drug dealer' looking type, anyway you get the gist he appeared to have the financial back up required for what I had in mind.

Smoking away, when it was still allowed on public premises, I told them I had a small venue in mind, less people, less hassle and only a few pals from each side present. No one getting in the way of the table, pure uninterrupted concentration for both players.

Snell cut to the chase "Per frame money or lump sum?"

"Lump sum, first to nine." I replied

"How much?" Snell asked.

"Well, that's what I've come to see you about" I stalled momentarily.

I wasn't sure if me and these guys had the same kind of numbers in mind or indeed the balls to back the finances up. Did this lad have 'real cash', would I get laughed at, or would it even worth the trip. I was no high roller, but I also didn't work for nothing, let's see how negotiations pan out.

"This is where you come good" Snell turned to his investor, the Black guy Des, "He has faith in me." Talking on Des's behalf.

"£500?" Snell probed, I knew that wasn't what 'd come for.

"Little bit more?" What I really meant was a 'LOTTLE' bit more, I hadn't come to piss around for £500, I could graft that in half a day if that's what I wanted.

"Were looking at quite a lump sum if possible" I replied

"As long as it's not stupid" Said Des.

"Summat in the region of £4,000" I waited for a response before continuing "First to 9, no start."

"Will you have some lads there that will have a bet with some of my lads?" Snell enquired.

The four grand wasn't a step too far, we were all just sounding each other out, £500 was their comfort blanket, but they knew as well as me it wasn't worth the organising.

"It's on" No more need for chit-chat just a time and a date to be confirmed. "Job done then, all the best lads, speak soon" and I was off.

Not wasting any time, and without even going home, I headed over to see some friends of mine, potential backers, not big black Des types, just local hard-working, well some of them, tradesmen from my area who I knew were doing alright for themselves and probably had a few grand hiding from the tax man under their mattresses. After a few awkward conversations to get the backing I needed I headed home and took my dogs out for a walk to clear my head, I was more than happy with the way this little venture was going and the fresh air would do me good.

The next day I headed off to meet another nice kid I knew from across town, he had a few quid and absolutely thought the world of Terry, when it came to pool, just like me he had no doubt in Terry's ability.

We met at the New Inn pub on Bernard Road, I had to square everything with the landlord as well for the venue. I'm not sure if we needed a license for this kind of thing, but in any event I wouldn't be getting one, I kept the game very hush, hush. I wanted things to remain very low key.

"Who's he playing?" Steve asked

"Kid from Chesterfield, Bob Snell, you heard of him?."

"No, but you haven't been wrong so far Clyde, I'll take your word, as I've never seen this lad play. Short frame span for that kind of money though mate" He quibbled, maybe trying to get me to re-think the arrangement.

"I'll make sure Terry gets his head down and practises. I'll make sure he stays off the ale and puts his concentration back into the pool." I reassured him.

As I was leaving I turned to the young lad Ben who was practising at the table and said "Just think in a few year you might be playing these kind of money matches, tha's definitely good enough." He smiled at me in agreement.

Little did we both realise, his idol, Terry would actually have him over further down the line, but I'd fix that.

I went back home and watched some of Terry's old videos on the trustee VHS. Reassuring myself of his abilities, looking for any small shortfalls in his play and style, to give him some advice. Advice? From me to a professional snooker player, who was I kidding, he could do it, I knew he could, first to nine, first to one, he was a different league to this lad Snell. Terry's professional record was something else.

Later that day it was straight across town to see yet another potential investor, ideally I wanted as few as possible to make up the four grand I needed, it was never going to be my four grand in the pot, whether I had faith in Terry or not, nothing would be left to chance.

We went down into my mate Steve's basement for the discussion, the lout was still half asleep, an opportune time to get him to sign up.

"Ranked number one in the world", I grinned, in the back of my mind knowing that was a historical statistic.

"I've got one backer at two grand, I was wondering if you wanted to put some up. I need the other two."

"I know the kid who he's playing. He tried to pass for the main tours and failed. Now Terry could still pass for the main tour easily" I aimed to reassure the guy, sell the investment opportunity at hand.

"What happens if he loses?" Steve asked, like he didn't know the answer.

Silly question I thought "Ye lose two grand."

"I'll chuck £500 in" Steve said.

"We don't want a lot of backers, we only want a small crowd not a lot of people know about it." I continued to pressure.

"No, I'll leave it." Second thoughts had hit him, probably along with a vision of his missus hitting the roof, back to the drawing board, but I would find someone.

Meanwhile I knew that Bob Snell was putting some serious hours in under the watchful eye of his investor Des. He was confident just like Terry, but not out of arrogance, he was putting the time in and his play was improving, he knew Terry's persona, he knew Terry probably, unless pushed, wouldn't bother.

"No prizes for second" Snell said, but Des his investor still looked worried. Remember he hadn't rounded up his four grand from the local estate, if Snell lost he lost the full wedge, so I can imagine how he was feeling, I'd been canny enough to spread my risk.

Again in my spare time I continued to watch more of Terry's match videos, in some respects training myself.

I headed off to the New Inn to have a few more discussions with the landlord, make sure nothing had changed, it was always best to reassure any element of the chain that may have second thoughts, the landlord, investors and even Terry, I didn't want any hiccups on the day.

"There won't be any trouble on the day?" The landlord asked.

"Worst comes to the worst I'll have to make a couple of phone calls, don't worry about that." I knew I wouldn't need to, unless Snell brought an army of Des's friends with him.

I went off to see another investor and moments later got the response I was looking for "If he puts the practise in I'll do it."

We were sorted the four grand was secured, now it was time to focus on the pool. I'd been out with my Harris Hawk again to relax and steady my nerves. Meanwhile back at his place Terry lay on the bed, trying to retain his composure. Match Day had arrived. I'd made my way round to Terry's place early. He looked nervous, making some toast like any other day, but now with the weight of the world, and four grand, on his shoulders.

THE FINALE

'Lousy Hunt'

It was crunch time, as we walked into the New Inn a small crowd were already waiting. They'd been looking forward to this day for the past month and had probably been camped outside overnight.

The black guy, Snell's backer, Des, turned up looking the part as ever, when moments later his credibility seeped through a grate in the floor as he pulled out a fucking cheque, was he taking the piss? I could only think that because the game was out of his area he was protecting himself from being mugged. We let it pass, knowing Snell would be the fall guy if it bounced.

We produced the cash, as you would expect, I gave the cheque the once over and then got the Landlord Mick to put both ends away in the safe. May the best man win!

Only about twenty people were present in total when the match took place, we didn't want any nonsense or rowdiness, there was way too much money down and way too much concentration required.

Terry was first to break, there was absolute silence.

A red went down from the break.

"Red ball potted" Said the makeshift referee.

The next one goes in and Terry clears up. A round of applause broke around the room, though it meant nothing at this stage, it was way too early in proceedings to gauge any outcome.

Terry-1, Bob-Nil

The ref racks them up again and it's Snell's turn to break.

One down but the white rolls in as well. It's Terry's turn to capitalise on Snell's poor stroke of luck.

Two more down but there's nowhere to go, he has to put Snell in a bad position, but the table is fast and it doesn't come off.

Snell to the table, he does the business and sees it through clearing up the lot.

Terry-1, Bob-1

Things start to pick up pace now, a few nervous sighs are exerted around the room to indicate the tension levels. Everyone has a few quid in this one, whether it be a grand or twenty quid, it was irrelevant, it all added to the tension.

Terry took the lead again.

Terry-2, Bob-1

Terry plays a poor shot, I shook my head, I had a few quid riding on the game myself, but pride was also on the line. I'd arranged the whole affair. Come on Terry for fucks sake!

Snell equalised and wandered over for a well earned sip of his pint, no one is daft enough to start throwing them ale down their neck when this kind of money is on the line, I can well see both men's pints lasting the full 9 frames.

Terry-2, Bob-2

The random nature of the game was starting to play on the minds of both player and a few discussions were had with the Ref, both players realising that 9 frames could simply fall on the side of luck. Like the old boy had said when we were organising the match, it was nothing, so they both agreed to play 'best of 25', first player to 13 wins. Throwing randomness out of the window. Who ever won now it would be a just victory and not the lay of the balls from the break making the decision. Something that had bewildered bar-room drunks for centuries, ruined many a bet and caused a few bar-room brawls over the years.

Terry cleared up from the next break, a great start for our man.

Terry-4, Snell-3

Terry sparked up a fag to steady his nerves, still avoiding his pint. These were still the good old days when you could kill yourself slowly at your own discretion and your friends around you, but everyone was happy.

The place was near silent, but for the occasional cry of encouragement "Come on Bob!" most likely desperation from watching their bets going down the pan. Terry was keeping his nose in front ... just!

Tery-6, Snell-4

But Bob was back on form, the black sinks, and Terry just can't shake him off. I started to regret every arranging this thing and putting my name, and other people's cash, on the line. The Carling was compensating a little, but also sending my mood in another direction. My head was shaking again, an involuntary sign that I wasn't happy, I didn't want Terry to realise, it was subliminal, nothing was going to stop it. Everyone else is the same, fumbling around, biting their nails, dragging down half cigs in one toke, all tell-tale signs of the working man's tension.

Terry-11, Snell-10

The game was picking up pace again.

Terry-11, Snell-11

Terry makes the perfect placement for the black in the middle bag ...

Terry-12, Snell-11

'ON THE HILL', The lad keeping scores scrawls onto the pub's chalk tally board. That's a Sheffield term indicating were on the verge of a win.

Snell lands a tight shot in the middle bag, almost a touching ball, but perfectly planted. I nearly choke back a whole cig in one drag, this game is so close you couldn't make it up, twelve a piece and they're both 'ON THE HILL' now.

I had to get up and stretch my legs, anyone could win the game now, I can't believe it's gone this far, I honestly thought it would be easy money when we'd first set about it. The crowd are looking visibly shattered never mind the players, like a Poker game that goes on late into the night, this one stops when it stops. Unbelievable.

The triangle is lifted from the rack for what might be one last time. Terry takes the break. A yellow sinks into the middle bag while Snell sinks into despair.

Terry fluffs the next shot, normally one he'd have put away without problem, "Fuckin hell" I mumbled, not at this stage, no room for errors now son.

Snell takes the table, sinks a Red. Terry is face down and rocking a little with the tension. He's hanging on by the skin of his teeth.

Snell fluffs it just like Terry, the moment getting to him, *Come on Terry,* hope is restored.

Terry chalks his cue for what seems like a good 30 seconds; preparation is everything now, every shot had to count, a glimmer of hope, he misses, but leaves Snell absolutely nothing!

Snell plays a soft shot to leave Terry in the mire, "Come on Terry" is all I can muster again, but Terry is lined up, and the next one, and the next one, just the yellow to go, but an awkward black remaining.

Don't go for this Terry I said to myself, as he goes for the double, softly, but it rattles around the pocket and rolls back out. Snell is back to the table and his supporters can see the finish line. He drops the first one a long way down the table "Reyt Shot!" three more and the black to go, my jaw is tight now, the tension is peaking.

Snell fluffs it, leaving Terry an easy pot on his last yellow, but still the awkward black. The white rolls up close to the black, a near impossible cut, but he goes for it, its shit or bust if he doesn't then Snell can capitalise, again it rattles around the corner pocket.

Snell pots one, then messes up the next, leaving Terry with what looks like an unmissable black, even I could put this one away, but the pressure of the occasion puts this easy shot up there with the hardest of his career.

No messing it's in, GET IN! That's why Terry had made it as far as he had, YEEESSSSS! A primeval roar around the table, applause coming from both sides. There's a relieved handshake between the players, there's no bad feeling from Snell, the game was so tough he doesn't even feel like a loser.

The black guy, his investor Des, looks destroyed, frozen in time, his expression doesn't change for nearly a minute.

Let's hope that fuckin cheque doesn't bounce son or it'll be a quick trip over to Chesterfield to make matters right I thought to myself.

It hits Snell after, sinking back into the New Inn backrest like he was being swallowed up.

It was over. Thank god. I headed back home and took the Hawk out one last time to unwind. What a fucking day.

* * * *

The match was well behind us but later on me and Terry Hunt had a small disagreement. The guy was genuinely tragic, I slowly began to realise that, a man who struggles with life, an amazing snooker player don't get me wrong, but as a human being he was useless, ever the victim, always revelling in his own personal tragedies, which weren't really tragedies by the way, you know the type.

Anyway as it happened he'd borrowed a cue from the young lad we knew form the pub, only about 16 years old, a promising young pool player by the name of Ben, a young lad who looked up to Terry.

After the Tournament the cue never came back, what a way to treat a young lad who looked up to you, his illusions shattered, but at sixteen year old he had no recourse, he couldn't tackle, or confront, a professional sportsman, that made no sense.

Anyway I'd heard first hand from Terry's missus that he'd sold the cue and frittered away the proceeds, again always thinking of himself and revelling in woe, sod poor Ben.

I'd put the word out for anyone who saw him to let me know, he wasn't in any of his usual haunts, but it wasn't going to take long for him to surface either. Even though I was willing to interject and help young Ben out I was too busy to spend my days looking for Terry myself. It was left down to time and a stroke of luck and sooner or later those things usually came together.

I'd started to see things in Terry Little dark sides, letting me down, telling me false truths, I could feel myself growing to dislike him, but selling Ben's cue was the icing on the cake.

Then one day out of the blue I got a call, "Terry Hunt's in the Shakespeare playing pool upstairs", So I rounded up a few pals, just in case, you never know who might want to look out for the local celebrity in the heat of the moment. Six of us shot down to the Shakespeare, all in separate cars, god knows what it must have looked like, a convoy of the local criminal fraternity racing through town.

The biggest lad in our firm shot straight in, stood in front of the crowd and scanned the room for Terry, I walked in behind, we spread out to scour the place, like searching for a rat in the dark.

"Where the fuck is he?" A bystander pointed him straight out. I hadn't even mentioned a name.

I walked straight over and steamed into him, another of the lads did exactly the same, the guy was screaming like a dog being kicked around a yard.

A little payback, but it didn't get young Ben his cue back, and funnily enough, still impressionable, Ben was sat there in the Shakespeare watching Terry play that day, ever the doting fan.

As I walked out I shouted, that was for you Ben and he gave me a little wink, *Cheers Clyde* he told himself. Silly really I could easily have gotten pulled for that, but he brought it about and it felt like justice had been served.

I've never spoke to Terry since. I still see him about from time to time, but that's done. Ted Bundy we used to call him, for his similar traits. Terry if you're reading this I hope your life is good, but you deserved that one, as I'm sure you'll agree.

MACHETE

'Life changing injuries, 2002'

Sometime after my final prison stint at Ranby something life changing happened to me. The title of the chapter and my lifestyle to date would probably suggest all out gangland warfare, a kidnapping maybe, though the outcome was much the same, the events which led up to it were not so glorious. You may have seen the horrific photos of my injuries on social media from a Machete attack, let's not kid anyone here it wasn't some long running gangland feud that escalated into me getting chopped up, I wasn't handcuffed to a radiator for days on end and tortured until I gave up the name of an associate, but more of a neighbourly dispute that got completely out of hand. I may make light of this now, but it did have life changing consequences for me, my family and my health and would you fucking believe it the bastard got a 'not-guilty'. I've had a couple of strokes of good luck in the courtroom, but this guy must have done something really special in a previous life.

Here's how it came about. Anyone who knows me knows I love my dogs. I've always kept them, even shown them in competitions, usually Pitbulls, rare breeds and working dogs. At the time I owned a Cane Corso Mastiff, mainly to protect my property, I'd called him Spike and I loved him dearly, he lived till about 12, god rest his soul.

Now if you don't know what a Cane Corso is, it's a big old beast, it's name derived from the Latin meaning "Protector", also known as the Italian Mastiff, it's a large Italian breed of dog, for years valued highly in Italy as a companion, guard dog, and hunter and usually weighing in the region of 45 to 50kg. If it decides it's doing something, you'd be pushed to stop it.

Unfortunately one day he'd managed to get out and caught site of an Alsatian across the road. The dog was being walked by a black guy from the estate. I'd seen him before but he wasn't really someone I knew well.

Spike was off like a rocket, he went for the other dog full on, straight over the road and tearing into the Alsatian before I could stop him. I ran over and managed to drag him off. I was over there like a shot and luckily managed to dissolve the situation before things had got out of complete control, you know the first few seconds where they're trying to dominate and not going full animal.

Anyway both dogs looked fine, I dragged Spike back to the house and gave him the obligatory 'telling off'. I made sure the yard was secure and carried on about my business. I'd brought my boy straight back home and thought little more of it. Maybe both dogs had taken a little nick, but there was nothing of significance to worry about or even warrant a trip to the Vets on either part.

About an hour or so later I heard a knock at the front door, something inside told me it was the dog owner coming to have words, that didn't bother me, I could hold my own verbally or otherwise and I knew there was no reason for any real problems. Yes it was my fault, it was my dog that had gotten out, but it was also a genuine accident and no real harm had been done, I thought.

I opened the door and there he was "Come and look at the injury to my dog," He griped.

Now I knew it was my fault so I'd have to entertain this fool for a spell, show a little concern, do what's right, that's all it would take. The guy only lived four or five doors away from us as it turned out. So I went round and he promptly pointed out a small hole in the dog's ear, a puncture wound if you could call it that, about as big as my thumb nail, the kind that most dogs forget about in about in an hour or so and has healed inside a couple of days, any dog owner would know that. I'm a dog lover myself, I knew it wasn't anything life threatening, if it was my dog it wouldn't need treatment, I'd maybe have cleaned it up as a matter of course but little else.

Again I'm out to appease the guy so I said "Fair enough, take it to the vet and let me know what I owe you", Trying not to sound too condescending at the same time.

At the end of the day it was an accident, but in some way my fault for not ensuring my dog was contained. At best I reckoned fifty quid, a couple of stitches, a course of antibiotics, straight in and out. Remember this was back in 2002, vets were on the take then as well, much like these days.

A couple of days later another knock came at the door, I instantly recognised it. The black guy had turned up again to 'deliver his invoice', so to speak. He said very little and handed me a bill for three hundred and sixty odd pounds.

I said "I'm not paying that, you must be fucking joking." He was lucky I was willing to pay anything at all and here was at my door again taking the piss.

He said "I had to leave it in for two nights".

"Why there were f*ck all wrong with it," Apart from the small tear, thumb nail sized, in his ear, nothing really.

He again asked "Are you gonna pay for it?" In a blunt Nigerian twang.

"Am I fuck." And went back into the house, still dumb founded by the nonsense I'd just been presented with.

Around this time I'd just bought a Nissan Pulsar GTR, you'd be pushed to find one these days, but let me tell you it shifted. It was an instant classic from the all-wheel drive turbocharged era. I've always loved my cars, and the kids loved this one too, because it shifted and I mean shifted. So I took them to McDonald's in it, ever the proud father, and then for a shoot down the M1 giving it some 'cosh' with the 360bhp under the bonnet being put to the test, it was an ex-rally car and really had some real poke.

As we pulled back up at our house we all got out. I saw the guy approaching. He asked again "Are you paying this bill or not?"

I again confirmed with an affirmative "Am I f*ck" That I wasn't.

He says "Right then" And walked off, like a man on a mission.

I'd presumed that was the end of it again for a few days and I carried on checking out my new car, the oil and the motor, just tinkering with my new pride and joy, when I heard my youngest lad Danny shout "Dad he's coming, he's got something in his hand". Bless you Danny for the tip off, looking out for his old man as always. But what was about to happen wasn't for any child's eyes.

I turned around and looked over as the guy approached me and saw, what I thought was, a little rounders bat down at his side. That didn't faze me either, yes I was at a disadvantage, but I doubt the fool would have the bravery to use it, how wrong I was.

I shouted to my boy "Don't worry about it, get yourself indoors son". Trying to appear clam for Danny's sake.

At that very moment he came at me, I'd told my little lad to get up the path but he wouldn't go, he wanted to look after his old man, he wanted to stay with me. The idiot came at me, swinging what I thought was the bat, aiming straight for my head, I quickly lifted my left hand to block it. Jackpot! I'd managed to block it and stop it from making contact with my head. In the same instance I let fly and smashed him full force with my right hand. It was a clean shot and had him straight down to the floor.

In that same swift movement I'd also managed to kneel on the bat to stop him from using it, it felt like it had scraped me on the way down, a strange sensation, except it wasn't a bat at all it was a fuckin Machete! If you've never seen one, it's a broad blade used for chopping, more like an axe. They were originally designed for agriculture, used to cut through rain forest undergrowth, but later adopted as the weapon of choice in many tropical countries, for uprisings, anyway this should never have been the weapon of choice for a black man residing in Sheffield, and boy was I about to find out how useful it had been in those uprisings.

I was knelt on the machete, but it was still in his hand, but as he went down from the swift right I'd given him, he'd sliced me down the bicep of my left arm, the adrenaline at that moment meant I was still fighting to get the better of him, and the horrific injury I'd suffered was something that I'd come to realise moments later.

I'd got him by the throat and just as I went to pull the trigger with my left arm and finish him off and let him have it with my left fist ... NOTHING! My hand just flopped back and I could feel it tearing away from the skin, like bark being stripped from a tree, there was nothing, absolutely nothing. I stopped mid brawl and looked at it, I still couldn't feel anything, my head couldn't work out what was going on, there was still no pain to confirm what I could see with my own eyes. Even my aggressor was taken aback, we both seemed to pause in time to take stock of my injuries, it was pure shock on both parts.

I looked down at the Machete and things started to fall into place, I'd been carved up like a Saturday 'Neet' Kebab.

My only regret about the whole thing was that I didn't turn this situation around. If I'd had my faculties about me I'd have taken the Machete from him and done him some real harm, removed some limbs, he'd brought this to me! Only a week before if I'd passed the guy in the street and even given him a neighbourly nod, being communal, how could something as crazy as this come about from something so trivial? He was older than me, I'd always assumed mild mannered, but obviously somewhere inside this guy was a deep, dark mean streak, crazy what hides behind your neighbour's door.

* * * *

An incident of that severity was never going to go under the radar, my injuries needed to be dealt with at the hospital and as expected the police were informed.

This wasn't gangland warfare, I wasn't on the receiving end of some vigilante hiding. I had no reason to help this guy out, or keep my mouth shut, and every reason to get my cut, excuse the pun, from the Criminal Injuries Board. I'd told the police what they needed to know and the guy was hauled in.

It was a clear cut series of events, and whether or not it was 'only' a dispute between neighbours that had boiled over, wandering about with a Machete meant one thing ... Gaol! And I had a few friends in there to help make amends, it was simply a matter of time.

Prosecutions and court dates take time, the availability of certain people, existing schedules etc. caused delays. Months passed and in those months my injuries meant I had to undertake some serious rehabilitation, in fact I still have very little movement in my left arm today. I spent a lot of time in physiotherapy to even get to the level of movement I have now. Those were difficult times, I was an active person generally, I wasn't used to having those kinds of physical restrictions holding me back.

I had physiotherapy for a total of 14 months, as well as occupational therapy, learning how to pick things up, putting shapes in their corresponding spaces like a child.

When it first happened I couldn't do anything, they'd fused my hand, if they hadn't it'd have looked completely deformed, repairing my tendons was an eleven and half hour operation. All the bones were smashed.

When the trial came around what occurred completely blew my mind. The guy got off scott free, I don't even want to go over the details of that, it happened and I needed to put it out of my mind for the good of my own sanity.

The guy eventually moved out of the area, without any assistance from me I might add, and we got on with family life. Revenge was always a waste of time for someone like me, I'd be straight back in the nick. Yes I still have a few problems associated with it, but it's long forgotten about, but certainly one of the more memorable times in my life.

UNDERWORLD AFTERWORLD

'Niche Nightclub'

My life continued to tootle down the criminal path, no major busts or sentences to speak of. My arm / hand still in recovery from the machete attack, but life was pretty straight forward and that's how I liked it.

I'd met a lot of faces from all across the country during my time inside, but I also knew of other serious names that operated down south in London. Though I'd never met many of them in the flesh, I knew a little about them from my conversations with Dave Lee and Sykesy. I knew who was worth the time of day and who wasn't.

Around the same time my brother in law Peter Skinner was organising paid tickets events up and down the country. If there was a niche and people were willing to pay to see it then he would arrange a suitable public speaking event. You know the type 'An Evening With', giving people a chance to meet their idols. When these events came to Sheffield then they would often take place at the Niche Nightclub, a place I knew only too well.

Niche has shut down now after a few unsavoury incidents involving drugs, guns and stabbings, but it was our place, we loved it and world famous for the evolution of bassline music, trust me it wasn't all bad, I was there.

One event my brother in law had put on was somewhat of a strange set-up of a show, on paper it shouldn't have worked, but it always sold out, it paid well and the punters loved it. He'd bring in celebrity gangsters from all around the country, usually the more infamous ones from London. This was before the dawn of internet, but people were still well aware of who these people were and the seriousness of their business. Obviously these guys were getting a little older now, winding down, and looking for easier ways to make a few quid. I was paid to look after them, pick them up, show them around town and make sure they were generally well looked after.

On one occasion we'd put on a bit of a show to raise some cash for charity, don't get me wrong everyone had to be paid and we had to make enough to cover our expenses, including drinks, but plenty was made to help local causes.

The 'faces' would travel up from London and tell some old school mob stories, these would include characters such as: Joey Pyle and Roy Shaw RIP etc. often accompanied by Tony Lambrianou, and on one occasion Freddie Foreman. The elite of London's, and indeed Britain's, underworld. All nice chaps I might add, but then I never had cause to see any other side of them.

When they came up to Sheffield I was the one employed to look after these guys, make sure they were well looked after, run them across town, just generally take care of them.

Being involved in this type of show a couple of times I knew the script off by heart. I'm not saying it was some kind of scripted pantomime, but without some structure it would have been a complete shambles you have to understand.

Anyway at given points, and sporadically, from time to time throughout the evening the audience were allowed to ask their own questions. I thought I'd use that opportunity myself, just like the next man, to get one in, wind up the lads, score a couple of points for the Northerners if you like, and my opportunity came.

"Roy, you were in jail with a pal of mine, Paul Sykes they called him ... " I directed my question at the infamous London hard man Roy Shaw. His face nearly hit the floor, it was a real picture.

"Whilst in the nick did you ever have any run-ins with my good pal Sykesy?" I continued, a wry grin across my chops, knowing that I half knew the answer already.

That one came to him as a shock to him, obviously I knew a little more than I was letting on. The infamous Joey Pyle quickly raised his hands and took the stance of an old school boxer, in a salute to good old Sykesy. The room remained silent.

I re-established myself "Sorry, I meant because of your personalities and the way you both were, did you ever come to blows or anything like that?" Clarifying my question.

Now to be fair to him, Roy came back with the perfect answer. Shaking his head "Paul was way too big for me" And we left it at that.

He knew I knew, and I knew what he meant. The audience were none the wiser. I'd heard more, but I wasn't going to push the subject, we were there to enjoy ourselves not generate aggro.

A few hours later we all went back to my mates Golf Club in Barlborough for a bit of an after party. I'd just walked into the toilet and there was Roy Shaw with the biggest bag of Charlie I think I've ever seen still in his hand, all for personal use you understand, and he went "Clyde do ye sniff?" With a cockney grunt.

I went "too fuckin right I do," And that was that, the party had started.

Ten minutes later, Roy asked "Is there anywhere more fackin lively'er than this?" He hadn't travelled all this way to hang out in the local club house.

I said "Come with me", I ordered taxis and we headed straight back into town back to the Niche Nightclub, me

Joey Pyle, Roy Shaw and Tony Lambrianou, you couldn't make it up.

Now they'd seen the Niche Nightclub earlier, but it wasn't the same one that I took them back to several hours later. It was transformed, it was a proper little ravers place, renowned across the country for its reputation as one of the best, and sometimes most dangerous, clubs in the country.

Some of the kids down there probably thought we were a bunch of old dummies, who'd stumbled into the wrong club, little did they know they were amongst gangland royalty.

Roy Shaw, nice as he was, was a menacing looking guy to be around, his eyes looked straight through you, he was wild behind those eyes. I heard an old Rampton tale that he was the only prisoner that they'd ever taken brain sample from, that's where we were at with this one, whether it's true I don't know, but his demeanour put the fear of god in to me and most, though he was perfectly nice in every instance in which I met him.

Everyone of those guys have now passed now, which is crazy, god bless. It seems like a lifetime ago and strange that none of them are still around, but still here I am, kicking around on the Manor.

Joey Pyle was the top man down there and again I found him to be the perfect gentleman.

At that time I was still recovering from the Machete attack, you can clearly see in the photos on social media from the time, my left hand still well and truly bandaged.

Around the same time my brother in law, Pete, had asked me to get Paul Sykes on board for those types of evenings. He would have been great at that, a natural public speaker, highly intelligent and had an opinion on everything. He was also not one to take any shit, no matter how big the crowd.

But by that time he'd already derailed somewhat, through drink and drugs. £2,000 for a few hours work, imagine that, what an opportunity lost. By then maybe already living on the streets, in fact I'd tried to find him, but in the end had to give up. I had visions of bumping into him, mid-flow in a heated debate with some randomer down the bus station, but I never found him, shame. Though at that stage maybe my name was better not put against him. For certain he'd have flattened a heckler or two and fallen over drunk on stage, the old Sykesy though, he'd have lapped it up, the crowd would have been hanging on his every word like a seasoned speaker / comedian holding the stage, god bless.

From there on the machete incident and all the time I'd spent in the nick had made me realise it just wasn't worth it anymore. Seeing the old school criminals coming up from London, some of them with little to their name made me realise that crime hadn't really paid for any us, but lord knows it had been an enjoyable rollercoaster, I decide to curb things and look to enjoy the steady life.

AFTERWORD

'Content with my lot'

I make no excuses for where my life went, my upbringing wasn't much different from the rest of the lads on the estates in Sheffield, but where I ended up over the years and the scrapes I got into, well those were my own doing.

I hope those kind of words don't mislead anyone, make no mistake I loved every minute of it, well nearly every minute of it, I have never really lived a life of regret, it's been colourful and I've met some great people along the way and without them I wouldn't be where I am today, content, with my loving family by my side.

Now this might sound ridiculous to some people, but I met some great people on the inside, who went on to become lifelong friends of mine and often business associates on the outside, such as Tommy Mason, Delroy Showers, Billy Barnes and Paul Sykes, not everyone was an out and out bad guy, some were unlucky and were there as a result of circumstance, some just knew no other way, like Paul, but they didn't necessarily have the devils blood running through their veins, I'm sure you understand what I am saying.

Some of the things that have happened feel like they are from another era, not a far cry from the tales of Sheffield's Gang War's portrayed by J P Bean.

I haven't been in trouble now since 1999. I still live on the Wybourn Estate, in the same house I've lived in for the last 20 years, and that's the way I intend for things to stay

The last time I was in prison was 1999 and I have no intention of going back. I've done a lot I've got away, despite my time in the nick, I still class myself as being a lucky criminally.

I have to be careful what I say, I'd hate to open any old wounds, but I'm in a different place now, far, far from the world I was in back then, let's not revisit that, but the feelings are still there. Have I changed? Have I fuck. I don't think I'll truly know myself until I'm dead and buried.

God bless, Clyde.

Also available from Warcry Press

'IT'S...
SHARKS!'

PAUL SYKES &
THE STRAITS OF JOHOR

The Adventures of Wakefield Born Boxer & Convict Paul Sykes. Including Guns, Gold & Sharks! The only man in the history of man-kind to swim across the Straits of Johor, nobody has ever done it before. Not because of the currents, or anything like that, It's... Sharks! Not shark infested, but of the locals go paddling there. "I know about Sharks, Yeah? Punch em right in the f*ckin ear ole and they swim off" Paul Sykes

A Short Story
by Rob Brenton ©